DIRECTORY of MASTER GLASS-PAINTERS

DIRECTORY
of
MASTER GLASS-PAINTERS

Edited by
BRIAN THOMAS and
EILEEN RICHARDSON

Oriel Press

© The British Society of Master Glass-Painters 1972

First published 1972

ISBN 0 85362 147 0
Library of Congress Catalogue Card No. 72-76380

Published for
The British Society of Master Glass-Painters
6 Queen Square, London, WC1N 3AR
by
ORIEL PRESS, Oriel Promotions Limited
32 Ridley Place
Newcastle upon Tyne, England, NE1 8LH

Printed by E. J. Arnold & Son Limited, Leeds

MODERN BRITISH GLASS

Stained glass is a craft which has preserved its grass roots. Hence its variety, for it reflects the tastes of a wide range of patrons. At one end of the scale, masterpieces of abstract and expressionist design, better than most to be seen on the continent, are widely disseminated in Britain. On the other hand, innumerable memorial windows in churches not only bear abundant evidence to an enduring piety, but also, by their tenacious traditionalism, are soon likely to be appreciated as a genuine aesthetic phenomenon. British glaziers can accommodate such individual demands because of their high technical proficiency and because their suppliers provide them with first-class materials. In the use of certain modern techniques, British designers have been in the vanguard. Hopes for the future are good, as a number of art colleges are giving a good training to talented and enthusiastic students.

The glazier's art, because it is strong and structural, is perhaps happiest in association with permanent buildings. That is why stained glass has come to be so closely associated with the Church, which is still unsurpassed in offering opportunities for deeply considered decorative work. But a tradition of secular glass is growing up, largely due to the Master Glass Painters' brochure "Extended Uses of Glass", which outlined the possibilities. Restaurants, factories, offices, museums, and trade fairs have all accepted the initiative, and there is every possibility that glass, exploiting the advantages of artificial light, may become a brilliant and fashionable mode of secular decoration.

A glory of glass is its colour, and it is a major handicap in producing a conspectus like this that colour reproduction is precluded by cost. Another handicap is that stained glass, being a form of architectural decoration, needs to be seen in its setting for the full appreciation of its scale, its pitch of tone and colour, and its stylistic aptness. (This last may be achieved either through harmonizing or through calculated contrast.) The value of the lists here published is that they proclaim the whereabouts of work by a substantial majority of the glaziers currently at work in Britain or in touch with this country. This and the previous Directories published by the British Society of Master Glass Painters will enable scholars and students to identify work, as well as adding to the interest of the sightseer.

As already suggested, one of the delights of stained glass is that it records a creative relationship between the artist and his patron. It seems likely that in the near future the Church will seek to satisfy the widespread yearning for some renewed form of spirituality by a more sophisticated metaphysical teaching. This offers unlimited scope for collaboration between priest and painter to devise a new symbolism, which will make religious buildings into shrines for meditation. Correspondingly, the industrialist, who has long recognized the potency of the poster for transient persuasion, might well humanize his buildings with visual symbols used as more permanent reminders of service to the community.

An application of stained glass which has hardly been explored is in the private house. At a cost no greater than would willingly be paid for a picture, a roundel of glass can be placed as a backlit wall panel, or let into a window, or even hung in front of existing plain glass. The interest of any house would be infinitely enhanced if the sequence of its occupiers could be visually recorded, especially if such records reflected individual interests and avocations. Greater domestic use could add another chapter to the long tradition of heraldic glass.

A word on the practicalities of commissioning stained glass may be helpful. A glazier may be brought into consultation for a small fee, and the patron may commission sketch proposals without further obligation. Glaziers tend to charge by the square foot and their prices differ as do those of other artists. But in the crafts, the "star" system does not as yet prevail to anything like the same extent as in painting and sculpture. There is much to be said for channelling negotiations through an architect, though most experienced glaziers can cope with all structural problems involved in installing glass. The permission of the local planning authority is required for additions to a scheduled secular building. Ecclesiastical work requires committee approval, first by the incumbent and his Parochial Church Council, then by the Bishop's Diocesan Advisory Committee and by the Diocesan Registrar, who grants a faculty for a statutory fee. An invaluable advisory body is the Council for the Care of Churches.

Readers of this Directory may be sufficiently interested in contemporary decorative glass to wish to become Lay Members of the British Society of Master Glass Painters. This they can do by applying to the Hon. Secretary, who will supply particulars. The Society continues its distinguished series of Journals. Recent books by members of the Society are:

Lawrence Lee: *Stained Glass* (O.U.P., 65p)
Patrick Reyntiens: *The Technique of Stained Glass* (Batsford)
Brian Thomas: *Geometry in Pictorial Composition* (Oriel Press, £3)

ABBOTT & CO. (LANCASTER) LTD.
R. F. Ashmead, FMGP
St. John's Studios, Chapel Street, Lancaster

LANCASHIRE

LANCASTER	*Priory Church*	1968	3-light window
FLEETWOOD	*Rossall School*	1965	3-light and tracery window

ABROAD

FRANCE

PERPIGNAN	*Museum of Religious Art*	1965	Single window

U.S.A.

STOW, MASSACHUSETTS	*St. Isadore's R.C. Church*	1964	Single circular window

St. Isadore's Roman Catholic Church, Stow, Massachusetts, U.S.A.

Above left
Museum of Religious Art, Perpignan, France.
Presented to the Town of Perpignan by the City of Lancaster
to mark the 'twinning' of the two towns in 1962.

Above right
Rossall School, Nr. Fleetwood, Lancashire.

Below left
Lancaster Priory Church, Lancaster.

JOSEPH BELL & SON STAINED GLASS
Geoffrey A. K. Robinson, AMGP
68 Park Street, Bristol BS1 5JX
Telephone : Bristol 28543

GLOUCESTERSHIRE
BRISTOL

ASHLEY ROAD	*St. Barnabas'*	1951	Main East Window
BARTON HILL	*St. Luke's*	1960–61	Three 2-light Apse windows
BEDMINSTER	*St. Aldhelm's*	1956	2-light window
	St. Paul's	1957	3-light East window
			3-light North Chancel window
BISHOPSTON	*St. Michael's*	1950	2-light War Memorial window
BRENTRY	*St. Mark's*	1971	Single-light in South Sanctuary window (cast glass and resin)
CITY	*Cathedral*	1950	South Transept South window re-arranged
			Four North Nave windows altered
		1951	Twelve Cloister windows incorporating ancient glass
	Christchurch	1956	3-light East window
			Four single light South Nave windows
	St. John the Baptist	1951	3-light North Chancel window
	St. Mary Redcliffe	1952–54	Repairing all stained glass windows
	St. Michael's	1951	2-light War Memorial window in South Aisle
		1954	2-light East window of South Aisle
	St. Stephen's	1951	6-light Main West window
	University	1953	21-light Founders' window
CLIFTON	*Christchurch*	1955	3-light Main West window
	Clifton College, North Town Oakfield Road	1953	3-light window
	Unitarian Church	1961	2-light South Nave window
FILTON	*Parish Church*	1967	5-light Main East window
	20 Pine Grove	1967	Single-light lounge window
HARTCLIFFE	*St. Andrew's*	1964	5-light South Sanctuary window (cast glass and resin)
		1969	Coloured glazing, North Wall (replacing 1963 window destroyed by fire)
HORFIELD	*Parish Church*	1950	2-light War Memorial window
KING SQUARE	*Deaf Institute Chapel*	1961	Multi-light East window
KNOWLE	*St. Martin's*	1953	Single-light South Aisle window
		1954	Central tracery in Main East window
		1959	Single-light South Aisle window
		1963	Two circular traceries in Main East window
LAWRENCE WESTON	*St. Peter's*	1963	One 3-light window and three multi-light windows
MONTPELIER	*Parkway Methodist Church*	1971	3-light East window (cast glass and resin)
REDLAND	*Highbury Congregational*	1952	4-light Main West window
	Redland Park Congregational	1957	3-light East window
			3-light West window
		1958	3-light South Nave window
	Tyndale Baptist Church	1955	Three 2-light Apse windows
			3-light North and South Transept windows
			2-light South Nave window

3

REDLAND (continued)	*Tyndale Baptist Church*	1955	Single-light Junior Church window
		1960	2-light South Nave window
		1971	2-light North Nave window
SHIREHAMPTON	*St. Mary's*	1962	3-light West Window War Memorial
SOUTHMEAD	*Hospital Chapel*	1961	Single-light East window
TWO MILE HILL	*St. Michael's*	1950	Main East window
WESTBURY ON TRYM	*Church of the Sacred Heart*	1953	Single-light Baptistry window
WHITCHURCH	*Counterslip Baptist Church*	1958	3-light East window

DEVONSHIRE

ASHREIGNEY	*Parish Church*	1964	Single-light West Porch window
CHITTLEHAMPTON	*Parish Church*	1955	4-light window in Gifford Chapel
WILLAND	*Parish Church*	1956	2-light window

DORSET

CHESILBOURNE	*Parish Church*	1956	3-light East window

GLOUCESTERSHIRE

PILNING	*Parish Church*	1951	Single-light North Nave window
STONE	*Parish Church*	1960	2-light North Nave window incorporating ancient glass
TUTSHILL	*St. Luke's*	1970	Single-light North Aisle window
WARMLEY	*Parish Church*	1950	Single-light Choir window

HAMPSHIRE

ROTHERWICK	*Parish Church*	1962	2-light South Transept window

HEREFORDSHIRE

WESTON UNDER PENYARD	*St. Lawrence's*	1955	2-light South Nave window

KENT

ELTHAM	*St. John the Baptist*	1952–3	Three single-light North Aisle windows
		1953	5-light East window
			4-light West window

LINCOLNSHIRE

GOSBERTON	*Parish Church*	1964	Single-light South Baptistry window
GREAT COATES	*Parish Church*	1962	2-light East window of Lady Chapel
		1969	3-light East window of North Aisle
SPALDING	*St. John's*	1957	Single-light South Aisle window

LONDON

CHARING CROSS	*Royal Commonwealth Society*	1951	Bristol Room window
WEST DULWICH	*All Saints*	1953	Two single-light Lady Chapel windows
		1956	Two single-light stairway windows

MONMOUTHSHIRE

PENALLT	*Old Church*	1969	Plain quarries restored and heraldry added to 3-light South Aisle window
			2-light West window

NORTHAMPTONSHIRE

DUSTON	*St. Francis*	1968	Four panels in four single-light windows of South Wall (cast glass and resin)

SOMERSET

ALCOMBE	*Grove Place Chapel*	1961–66	3-light East window
		1965	Single-light South Sanctuary window
BANWELL	*Parish Church*	1966	15th to 18th century glass in 3-light East windows of North and South Aisles restored and set on plain quarries
BATH	*Abbey*	1949–53	Two 4-light East windows of North and South Aisles 5-light North Nave window Repairs and adaptations to twelve clerestory windows over Vestry and South Aisle
	Prior Park College	1966	Single-light window in classroom block
	St. Stephen's	1953	2-light Nave window
BERROW	*St. Mary's*	1970	3-light West window
BITTON	*Parish Church*	1952	2-light window
BRIDGWATER	*St. Mary's*	1955	3-light West window of South Aisle
		1958	3-light West window of North Aisle
BROCKLEY	*Parish Church*	1952–4	Repairs to all windows painted by W. R. Eginton
CATCOTT	*Parish Church*	1953	East window
CHILTON TRINITY	*Parish Church*	1958	3-light East window
CLAVERTON	*Parish Church*	1958	Repairs to two 3-light windows of ancient glass
CLEVEDON	*St. Andrews*	1956	2-light window in South Transept
		1958	2-light South Chancel window
		1960	2-light North Chancel window
	27 Dial Hill Road	1968	Interior Screen (cast glass and resin)
COMPTON BISHOP	*Parish Church*	1958	2-light South Chancel window
CONGRESBURY	*Parish Church*	1958	East window altered, ancient glass in tracery restored
CURRY MALLET	*Mallet Court*	1965	Single-light staircase window incorporating 15th to 17th century panels
HAM GREEN	*Hospital Mortuary*	1970	Single-light window (cast glass and resin)
HENTON	*Parish Church*	1960	Single-light South Chancel window
LEIGH WOODS	*St. Mary's*	1961	2-light North Nave window
NAILSEA	*Parish Church*	1955	3-light East window
PILL	*Christ Church*	1958	3-light East window Single-light West window of St. James' Chapel Single-light South Nave window
STOKE-SUB-HAMDON	*Parish Church*	1953	Single-light North window
TAUNTON	*St. Margaret's (Somerset Guild of Craftsmen)*	1963	Single-light window in Chapel
	Silver Street Baptist Church	1956	2-light South Aisle window
		1959	Two 2-light South Aisle windows
WESTON SUPER MARE	*Emmanuel Church*	1957	East window altered
	St. Saviour's	1957	Single-light South Aisle window
WORLE	*Crematorium Chapel*	1965	Multi-light South window

SURREY

GUILDFORD	*Methodist Church*	1966	Multi-light Entrance window

SUSSEX

BURWASH	*Parish Church*	1955	2-light South Aisle window

WARWICKSHIRE

EARLSWOOD	*Methodist Church*	1960–61	3-light West window

WILTSHIRE

CHIPPENHAM	*St. Paul's*	1971	2-light South Aisle window (designed by Roger Fifield, AMGP)
LYDIARD TREGOZ	*Parish Church*	1969	15th century heraldry restored and placed in 3-light South window of Chapel
LYDIARD MILLICENT	*Parish Church*	1970	15th century fragments restored and placed in 3-light West window of South Aisle
RAF LYNEHAM	*St. Joseph's R.C. Church*	1968	All windows (cast glass and resin) Christus Rex (leaded)
OAKSEY	*Parish Church*	1963	Single-light South Nave window
SALISBURY	*St. Thomas*	1966	15th century glass restored and placed in 3-light South window of Lady Chapel Restoration of 14th century traceries in North Ambulatory window
SWINDON	*St. Augustine's*	1955	Single-light South Aisle window
		1961	Single-light South Aisle window
	St. Barnabas	1954	Single-light North Aisle window
		1962	Single-light North Aisle window
		1965	Single-light North Aisle window
		1968	Single-light North Aisle window
		1970	Single-light North Aisle window

WORCESTERSHIRE

BROADWAY	*Parish Church*	1950	Single-light window of ancient glass

EIRE

DUBLIN	*T. G. Wilson, Esq.*	1962	Heraldic Panel

ABROAD

SWITZERLAND

VISP	*Spital St. Maria*	1961	Panel in Hospital Entrance

Opposite
Left
Ashreigney Parish Church, Devonshire.

Top right
St. Francis' Church, Duston, Northamptonshire.

Bottom right
The Old Church, Penallt, Monmouthshire.

All designs opposite by Geoffrey Robinson.

IN LOVING MEMORY OF
MARY JANE BOUNDY
1962

BERKSHIRE

DORNEY NEAR WINDSOR	*Church of St. James*	1965	Memorial window in Nave

ESSEX

THUNDERSLEY	*Church of St. Peter*	1966	24 feet high inclined windows to North and South of Sanctuary

LONDON

GREEN STREET W1	*Film Production Assoc. of Great Britain*	1968	Large Chandeliers to Committee and Conference Rooms
HAMPSTEAD	*Post House Hotel Trust Houses Group*	1970	Four large interior screens to entrance Bar and Restaurant. Double sided glass applique
	Post House Hotel Trust House Forte	1971	Extra screen to above scheme
KENSINGTON W14	*Private residence*	1966	Three windows to private chapel
KENSINGTON SW5	*Private residence*	1970	Plain glazed window to staircase in open plan entrance
NORTH AUDLEY STREET W1	*La Napoule Restaurant*	1969	Sandblast engraved mirrors and glass screens with bright and grey silvering. Internally lit decorative banister rods. Light fittings
PICCADILLY W1	*Hatchetts Restaurant*	1967	Three large interior screens of double sided glass applique between Restaurant and Playground areas
	Hatchetts Dover Street	1967	Engraved mirror for Yardley
PORTLAND PLACE W1	*Town Planning Institute*	1965	Engraved mirror in vestibule

SUSSEX

EASTDENE	*Collectors private residence*	1962	Plain glazed and sandblasted interior screen with superimposed free standing glass construction
SELMESTON	*Private residence*	1962	Glass applique garden door

ABROAD

FRANCE

OUISTREHAM, NORMANDY	*Church of St. Samson*	1964	Commando Memorial window

GHANA

KUMASI, ASHANTI	*Ashanti Palace*	1971	Engraved mirror doors, bright and grey silvering with sandblast and brilliant cut engraving

Opposite
Top left and right. Church of St. Peter, Thundersley, Essex.
North Sanctuary window. Section symbolising events in life of St. Peter *(left).*
South Sanctuary window. Section symbolising Keeper of the Keys of Heaven *(right).*

Below. The Post House Hotel, Hampstead, London, N.W.3

Above and Below
La Napoule Restaurant, North Audley Street, London, W.1

KENNETH GORDON BUNTON, AMGP
Eagle Lodge, Marlpit Hill, Edenbridge, Kent

DEVONSHIRE
STAVERTON   *Parish Church*   1962   3-light stained glass Resurrection

KENT
FOLKESTONE   *St. Oswald, Paddlesworth* 1966   One single-light slab glass and concrete Ascension

LANCASHIRE
MANCHESTER   *Christ Church, Davyhulme*   1969   Four single-lights, slab glass and concrete

LONDON   *Congregational Church of the Growing Light*   1968   Slab glass and concrete

WARWICKSHIRE
BIRMINGHAM   *St. Peter's, Tile Cross*   1967   Christ the Mediator 5-light stained glass
Four Chapel windows and Saints

YORKSHIRE
LEEDS   *Holy Trinity*   1970   Slab glass and concrete, single-light. The Trinity

ABROAD

NEW ZEALAND
PALMERSTONE NORTH   *St. Peter's*   1964   Five single-light Clerestory Stained glass. Five Saints

SOUTH AFRICA
TRANSVAAL   *Umkomaas*   1967   Three single-light stained glass Three Angels

St. Peter's, Palmerston North, New Zealand. Baptismal Window.

11

Above. St. Peter's Church, Tile Cross, Birmingham, Warwickshire.
St. John *(left)* and Christ the Mediator *(right).*
Below left. Christ Church, Davyhulme, Manchester, Lancashire. Crucifixion.
Below right. Holy Trinity, Leeds, Yorkshire. The Trinity.

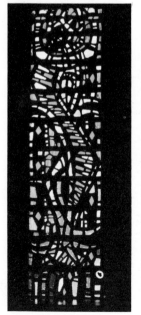

CELTIC STUDIOS
Hubert P. Thomas, MGP   Howard Martin, MGP
5 Prospect Place, Swansea, Glam., SA1 1QP

CHESHIRE

COPPENHALL, CREWE	*St. Michael's*	1968	Single-light Nave window
BIRKENHEAD	*St. James'*	1969	2-light Lady Chapel window

DEVONSHIRE

COLLATON	*St. Mary's*	1964	Single-light window

HEREFORDSHIRE

CLEHONGER	*All Saints'*	1964–68	3-light Lady Chapel window Restoration of 3-light East window 3-light East window, South Aisle
BREINTON COURT		1968	Heraldic Arms
GLASBURY-ON-WYE	*St. Peter's*	1965	Two single-light West windows faceted slab glass set in resin matrix

LONDON

CROYDON	*Viscose Development Co. office block*	1963	Interior Screen in faceted slab glass in resin matrix
HOUNSLOW	*Holy Trinity Church*	1964–69	Large 5-light Sanctuary window 3-light Baptistry window

MONMOUTHSHIRE

EBBW VALE	*Christ Church*	1953–67	4-light West window 2-light Nave window
LLANARTH	*St. Teilo's*	1970	3-light East window
MOUNTAIN ASH	*St. Margaret's*	1961	2-light Nave window
PONTNEWYNYDD	*St. Luke's*	1964	Three single-light Nave windows
ROGGIET	*St. Mary's*	1961–66	Two 3-light Nave windows North Wall 2-light Nave window South Wall
RISCA	*St. Mary's*	1970	3-light Chancel window North Wall

SOMERSET

COMBWICH	*St. Peter's*	1970	Restoration of West window

STAFFORDSHIRE

WOLVERHAMPTON, OXLEY	*Church of the Epiphany*	1964 1970	Single-light Transept window 3-light Nave window

WALES

ANGLESEY

LLANDONNA	*St. Dona*	1964	3-light East window

BRECONSHIRE

BWLCH	*All Saints*	1951–67	2-light East window and single-light West window
CRAY	*St. Ilid*	1960	Single-light East window
LLANELLY	*St. Ellyw*	1968	3-light East window

CARDIGANSHIRE

YSBYTY YSTWYTH	*St. John Baptist*	1962	East and Chancel windows
VELINDRE	*St. Barnabas*	1963–67	Three single-light Nave windows and Restoration of West window
BORTH	*St. Matthews*	1963–67	Single-light Nave window Two 2-light Nave windows 2-light West window

CARDIGANSHIRE (continued)

LLANDRE	*Parish Church*	1966	Single-light Nave window
SILIAN, LAMPETER	*St. Sulien*	1961–70	Two single-light Nave windows
LLANILAR	*St. Mary's*	1961–67	3-light East window
			2-light Nave window
			Single-light Chancel window
CILGERRAN	*Parish Church*	1970	Two 2-light Nave windows
HENLLAN	*St. David's*	1967	Single-light Chancel window

CARMARTHENSHIRE

BETTWS, AMMANFORD	*Dewi Sant*	1962	2-light Nave window
BURRY PORT	*St. Mary's*	1960–64	Two 2-light Nave windows
PONTYATES	*St. Mary's*	1954–63	Two 2-light Nave windows
MYDRIM	*Parish Church*	1965	2-light Nave window
LLANLLWCH	*St. Mary's*	1952–69	3-light East window
			2-light Nave window
			Single-light Chancel window
CWMGORSE	*St. Mary's*	1956–70	2-light East window
			2-light West window
			Single-light Baptistry window
			Five single-light Nave windows
CWMFFRWD	*St. Anne's*	1962	2-light Nave window
BRYNAMMAN	*St. Catherine's*	1957	2-light Nave window
DAFEN	*Parish Church*	1966	2-light Chancel window
PEMBREY	*St. Illtyds*	1958–69	2-light Nave window
			3-light Lady Chapel window
LLANGUNNOR	*St. Ceinwrs*	1969	2-light Nave window
LLANFYNYDD	*Parish Church*	1969	3-light Baptistry window
KIDWELLY	*Parish Church*	1960	5-light West window
FERRYSIDE	*St. Thomas*	1965	3-light Transept window
TUMBLE	*Dewi Sant*	1965	3-light Transept window

FLINTSHIRE

BUCKLEY	*St. Matthew's*	1967	3-light Nave window
PRESTATYN	*Church of the Holy Spirit*	1969	6-light Sanctuary window

GLAMORGANSHIRE

ABERAVON	*St. Mary's*	1965	2-light Lady Chapel window
ABERFAN	*New Church*	1970	4-light window
BRITON FERRY	*St. Clement's*	1962	3-light Transept window
			2-light Nave window
BRITON FERRY LLANSAWEL	*St. Mary's*	1966	Single-light Nave window
BARGOED	*St. Gwladys*	1966	Single-light Chancel window
CRYNANT	*St. Margaret's*	1951–66	3-light East window
			Ten 2-light Nave windows
			2-light Baptistry window
CARDIFF, CYNCOED	*All Saints'*	1964	Single-light Chapel window
CARDIFF	*Park End Presbyterian Church*	1967	3-light Chancel window
CARDIFF, PARK END	*Presbyterian Church*	1967	3-light Chancel window
CARDIFF, RADYR	*Christ Church*	1968	3-light Nave window
CARDIFF	*New Synagogue*	1966	3-light Faceted Slab Glass in Resin Matrix
CWMAVON	*St. Michael's*	1964	2-light Chancel window
DINAS POWIS	*St. Peter's*	1970	Single-light Baptistry window
FOCHRIW	*St. Mary's*	1962–66	3-light East window
KILLAY	*St. Hilary's*	1964	2-light Nave window
KENFIG HILL	*St. Theodore's*	1957–65	Two 2-light Nave windows
LLANMAES	*St. Cadoc's*	1950–65	Two 3-light Nave windows

LLANBRADACH	Parish Church	1969	2-light West Aisle window
MORRISTON	St. John's	1961	3-light East window
MERTHYR TYDFIL	St. David's	1969	Restoration of single-light Chancel window
	St. Tydfil's	1970	Restoration of West window
NEATH	St. David's	1961–68	2-light Nave window
			Two single-light Nave windows
			2-light West Aisle window
	St. Catherine's	1969	Single-light Nave window
PORT TALBOT	St. Agnes	1950–66	3-light East window
			Single-light Lady Chapel window
			3-light West window
PONTYPRIDD	Crematorium Church	1964	3-light Chapel window
PORT EYNON	St. Catwg	1955–62	Four single-light Sanctuary windows
			3-light Nave window
RESOLVEN	St. David's	1955–69	Five single-light Nave windows
			Single-light Porch window
SWANSEA	St. Michael's	1947	5-light East window
	St. Gabriel's	1960–69	4-light West window
			2-light Chapel window
			2-light West window, North Aisle
	St. Jude's	1949–68	7-light West window
			Three 2-light Nave windows
	St. Barnabas	1964	Two 3-light Chancel window
			Single-light Sanctuary window
	St. Luke's	1968	3-light West window
			Single-light West Aisle window
	St. Peter's Newton	1968	5-light West window
SKEWEN	St. John the Baptist	1952–63	Two single-light Baptistry windows
			Three 2-light Nave windows
TREBANOS	St. Michael's	1956-67	Five Nave windows
YSTRADGYNLAIS	St. Cynog's	1969	Single-light Nave window
YSTALYFERA	St. David's	1967	2-light Nave window

MONTGOMERYSHIRE

DOLANOG	Parish Church	1965	3-light East window
WELSHPOOL	St. Mary's	1970	Restoration to Nave windows

MERIONETHSHIRE

MAENTWROG	St. Twrog	1964	2-light Nave window
HARLECH	St. Tanwg	1965	Single-light Nave window

PEMBROKESHIRE

JOHNSTON	Parish Church	1968	Single-light East window
ST. TWYNNELLS	Parish Church	1970	Single-light Chancel window
FISHGUARD	St. Mary's	1954	2-light Nave window
		1970	Circular Narthex window
			2-light Nave window
BURTON	Parish Church	1967	2-light Nave window
HAVERFORDWEST	St. Mary's	1964–70	Single-light West Wall window
			Restorations to East and West windows
AMBLESTON	Parish Church	1965	3-light East window
WALTON EAST	St. Mary's	1967	Single-light Chancel window
LLANDELOY	St. Teilo	1965	Single-light Nave and small West window

RADNORSHIRE

LLANDRINDOD WELLS	Holy Trinity	1970	Large 3-light West window
	St. Michael's	1967	3-light East window

CANADA
PROVINCE OF ALBERTA

RED DEER	*Gaetz Memorial United Church*	1957	Main 3-light Chancel window
EDMONTON	*St. John the Evangelist*	1963 1969	Baptistry window Two single-light Sanctuary windows

PROVINCE OF BRITISH COLUMBIA

VANCOUVER	*St. Margaret's Anglican Church*	1959 1968	Single-light Nave window Single-light Nave window
VANCOUVER ISLAND	*Duncan United Church*	1967	Two single-light windows
VANCOUVER, OAK BAY	*St. Mary's*	1960–64	Complete set of twenty-one Nave windows
PENTICTON	*St. Saviour's*	1962–65	3-light East window 2-light Nave window

PROVINCE OF MANITOBA

WINNIPEG	*St. Andrew's River Heights United Church*	1953 1964	Large 3-light Chancel window 9-Narthex windows
THE PAS	*Westminster United Church*	1966	Single-light Nave window

NEWFOUNDLAND

DEER LAKE	*St. Paul's United Church*	1967	Circular East window

PROVINCE OF ONTARIO

ALLANDALE	*St. George's Anglican Church*	1965–69	Two 2-light Nave windows
BRANTFORD	*Brant Avenue, United Church*	1957–66	West window Chapel window Single-light Nave window
BALFOUR	*United Church*	1970	Single-light window
GREGORY, MUSKOKA	*Christ Church*	1961–62 1971	Two single-light Nave windows Single-light Nave window
HAMILTON	*Church of the Redeemer International*	1966	Single-light window
PURCELL'S COVE	*St. Phillip's*	1967	Single-light window
PORT NELSON	*Port Nelson United Church*	1963–68	Eight Clerestory windows in a scheme of twelve windows
PRESTON	*St. John's Anglican Church*	1959–70	3-light West window Eleven Nave windows from a scheme of eighteen windows
ST. MARY'S	*St. James' Church*	1969	2-light Nave window
LINDSAY	*Cambridge United Church*	1969	2-light Narthex window
SARNIA	*Canon Davis Memorial Church*	1960–68	Two 2-light Nave windows West Wall Rose window
RENFREW	*St. Andrew's United Church*	1966	Two single-light Nave windows
TORONTO	*Runnymede United Church*	1960–69	Twelve 4-light Nave windows 2-light Narthex window
	Runnymede Presbyterian Church		2-light East window
	Bloor Street United Church	1959–61	9-light Great West window Nine Narthex windows Two Main Entrance windows
	Birchcliffe Heights United Church	1964–70	2-light Nave window Two single-light Nave windows
	St. George's-on-the-Hill	1965	3-light Transept window
WELLAND	*Central United Church*	1969	2-light Nave window
WESTON	*Presbyterian Church*	1967–69	Six 2-light Nave windows from a scheme of ten Nave windows
OTTAWA	*Uplands R.C.A.F. Chapel (R.C.)*	1964	Baptistry and 2-light Nave window

PROVINCE OF QUEBEC

MONTREAL	*Trinity Memorial Church*	1968	Large 5-light Gallery window
	Greenfield Park, St. Paul's	1969–70	Two 2-light Nave windows
	Church of the Annunciation (R.C.)	1958–61	2-light Chancel window Four Clerestory windows Two large 3-light Transept windows
	Lachine, St. Andrew's Presbyterian Church	1961–66	Four 3-light Nave windows
	Hampstead, St. Matthew's	1965	3-light West window Five single-light Narthex windows
	Mount Royal Crematorium Chapel	1964	3-light window

PROVINCE OF SASKATCHEWAN

REGINA	*First Presbyterian Church*	1960–64	Two 2-light Nave windows 3-light Transept window
SASKATOON	*Cathedral Church of St. John*		Single-light Nave window

SOUTH AFRICA

CAPE TOWN	*Greenpoint, St. Alban's*	1960–66	Three single-light Sanctuary windows Single-light Nave window
	Sea Point, St. James'	1964–67	3-light Lady Chapel window Tracery sections of East window
	St. George's Cathedral	1971	Single-light window
TRANSVAAL	*Brakpan, St. Peter's*	1968–70	Complete scheme of seven Nave windows
HEIDELBERG	*Parish Church*	1965	Rose window, All Soul's Chapel

WEST INDIES

TRINIDAD	*Pointe-a-Pierre, St. Peter's*	1966	Large Circular East window
JAMAICA	*Milk River, St. Saviour's Church*	1968	Large Circular window

U.S.A.

PHILIPSBURG	*St. Paul's*	1967	Single-light Nave window
BATAVIA, N.Y.	*St. James'*	1960–65 1969	Ten 2-light Nave windows 2-light Clerestory window
MINNEAPOLIS	*Cathedral Church of St. Mark*	1971	2-light large Nave window

FREDERICK W. COLE, RF, FMGP
Cerne House, Nonington, nr. Dover, Kent

BERKSHIRE

PANGBOURNE	*Naval College Chapel*	1951	3-light Chancel

BUCKINGHAMSHIRE

FARNHAM COMMON	*St. Johns Church*	1947	Single-light South Aisle
		1948	Single-light West window
		1951	2-light North Aisle
		1957	2-light North Aisle
STOKE POGES	*Parish Church*	1957	Single-light Chapel

CAMBRIDGESHIRE

MADINGLEY	*U.S.A. Cemetery Chapel*	1955	Heraldic windows

CHESHIRE

OVER PEOVER	*St. Lawrences Church*	1951	2-light South Aisle
LISCARD	*St. Thomas's Church*	1952	3-light Lady Chapel

CORNWALL

PENZANCE	*St. Johns Church*	1955	3-light West window

DERBYSHIRE

MELBOURNE	*St. Michael's Church*	1952	Single-light Narthex
MELLOR	*St. Thomas's Church*	1955	3-light Belfry

DORSET

H.M.S. MAIDSTONE	*Chapel*	1949	3-light North Aisle

DURHAM CO

SUNDERLAND	*Mission to Seamen*	1950	2-light North Aisle
		1951	4-light East Chancel
		1952	2-light South Aisle
		1957	2-light South Aisle

ESSEX

ABRIDGE	*Holy Trinity Church*	1954	3-light East window
MALDON	*All Saints Church*	1950	3-light South Aisle
CHIGWELL	*St. Mary's Church*	1959	2-light South Aisle

GLOUCESTERSHIRE

ARLINGHAM	*St. Mary's Church*	1949	2-light North Chancel

HEREFORDSHIRE

HEREFORD	*All Saints Church*	1949	Single-light Lady Chapel
		1950	3-light North Aisle

HERTFORDSHIRE

HARPENDEN	*St. John's Church*	1964	Two 2-light Lady Chapel

KENT

EASTRY	*Parish Church*	1965	3-light Baptistry
BARMING	*Parish Church*	1968	Single-light South Aisle
			Two Porch windows
FOLKESTONE	*Trinity Church*	1968	2-light window North Aisle
		1970	2-light window North Aisle
TEMPLE EWELL	*Parish Church*	1970	Porch window
THANINGTON WITHOUT	*St. Nicholas' Church*	1970	Chapel window

LANCASHIRE

STAND	*Unitarian Church*	1954	3-light East window
			Single-light Chapel
		1956	Single-light South Aisle

LONDON

CLAPHAM	*Christchurch*	1950	3-light East window
COMMERCIAL ROAD	*British Sailors Society*	1963	Single-light East window
HATCHAM	*St. Catherine's Church*	1953	3-light East window
LEE	*St. Mildred's Church*	1953	10-light Chancel Apse
BROMLEY BY BOW	*All Hallows Church*	1956	5-light Apse
STREATHEM	*St. Leonard's Church*	1959	2-light North Aisle

MIDDLESEX

TEDDINGTON	*St. Alban's Church*	1953	3-light Chancel window
			Clerestory windows

NORFOLK

HEIGHAM	*St. Thomas's Church*	1956	3-light East window

NORTHAMPTONSHIRE

COLLINGTREE	*St. Columbas Church*	1955	2-light Chapel East

STAFFORDSHIRE

HIGH OFFLEY	*St. Mary's Church*	1950	Two 3-light South Aisle
		1951	Two 3-light South Aisle

SUSSEX

HORSTED KEYNES	*St. Giles Church*	1950	Single-light North Aisle

SURREY

NEW ADDINGTON	*St. Edward's Church*	1960	Single-light North Aisle
MITCHAM	*Church of the Ascension*	1952	3-light West window
			Baptistry window
HINCHLEY WOOD	*St. Christopher's Church*	1958	Single-light North Aisle
		1958	3-light Chapel window
		1960	Single-light
GATTON PARK	*Royal Alexandra*	1958	Single-light East window

YORKSHIRE

HONLEY	*St. Mary's Church*	1952	Single-light East window
		1969	Single-light Aisle window
BIRKBY	*St. John's Church*	1950	5-light West window
			3-light North window
			3-light South window
HAWKSWORTH	*St. Mary's Church*	1953	2-light Baptistry
PENISTONE	*Church of St. John the Baptist*	1951	3-light South Aisle window
WOODKIRK	*Church of St. Mary the Virgin*	1963	2-light North Chancel
		1966	2-light North Aisle
THORNE	*Parish Church*	1964	Single-light South Aisle
GILDERSOME	*St. Peter's Church*	1965	Great west window
		1966	All South Aisle windows
MILNSBRIDGE	*St. Luke's Church*	1966	North Chancel window

CHANNEL ISLANDS

JERSEY	*St. Andrew's Church*	1949	3-light West window
FIRST TOWER		1951	3-light South Aisle

NORTHERN IRELAND

BELFAST	*Christ Church*	1959	Single-light
	St. Katherine's Church	1960	Circular window
	St. James' Church	1952	3-light East window
	Holy Trinity Church	1955	5-light East window
	St. Peter's Church	1950	5-light North Transept
LISBURN	*Christchurch Cathedral*	1950	5-light East window

WALES

ABERGAVENNY	*Church of St. Mary the Virgin*	1957	5-light West window
ST. DAVID'S	*St. David's Cathedral*	1957	Two Rose windows
OXWICH	*St. Illtyds Church*	1968	Single-light South Aisle
LLANGOED	*Penmon Church*	1968	2-light South Aisle

ABROAD

AUSTRIA
VIENNA	*Christ Church*	1949	3-light East window Eighth Army Memorial

CANADA
PRINCE EDWARD ISLAND	*St. Peter's Cathedral*	1950	Single-light
RIVERSIDE	*United Church*	1958	3-light East window
STELLARTON	*Sharon United Church*	1956	3-light East window
CHARLOTTETOWN	*St. Peter's Church*	1948	Single-light South Aisle
WINNIPEG	*St. Andrew's Church*	1955	2-light Choir

ICELAND
BESSASTADIR	*Presidents Church*	1949	Single-light East window
		1957	All Aisle windows
AKUREYRI	*Lutheran Church*	1960	5-light West window

NEW ZEALAND
AUCKLAND	*St. Matthew's Church*	1951	4-light West window
TAUPO	*St. Andrew's Church*	1949	3-light East window

NORTH AFRICA
TUNIS	*St. George's Church*	1950	Single-light Aisle window

RHODESIA
CASTLE ZONGA	*St. Peter's Church*	1950	Single-light North Aisle
WEST NICHOLSON	*Railway Mission*	1950	Single-light East window

SOUTH AFRICA
DORDRECHT	*St. Augustines Church*	1950	Single-light East window
PORT ELIZABETH	*Holy Trinity Church*	1951	2-light South Aisle
		1970	2-light North Aisle
SEA POINT	*St. James' Church*	1955	2-light South Aisle
KIMBERLEY	*Boys High School*	1957	Library window
SWARTKOPS	*St. Agnes' Church*	1960	Circular window
IDUTYWA	*St. Barnabas' Church*	1965	Single-light Aisle
CATHCART	*St. Alban's Church*	1965	Single-light Aisle
		1966	Three single-light Aisle
BENONI	*St. Dunstan's Church*	1966	Single-light Aisle
KING WILLIAM'S TOWN	*St. Katherine's Church*	1966	Single-light Aisle
VINCENT	*St. Alban's Church*	1968	All windows
STRAND	*St. Andrew's Church*	1970	Single-light Aisle
RANDFONTEIN	*St. John's Church*	1968	Single-light Aisle
RONDEBOSCH	*St. Thomas' Church*	1962–71	Five single-light Aisle Three single-light Chapel
	Congregational Church	1971	Single-light Aisle

SOUTH ATLANTIC
ST. HELENA	*St. Paul's Cathedral*	1950	2-light South Aisle

UGANDA
M'BARARA	*St. James' Church*	1950	3-light East window

U.S.A.

EVANSVILLE	*Church of the Redeemer*	1956	3-light East window
HOUSTON	*Trinity Lutheran Church*	1954	All windows
	St. John the Divine Church	1966	Seven 2-light windows
PAMPA	*St. Matthew's Church*	1955–57	Two 2-light Aisle
		1963–65	Four single-light Aisle
DALLAS	*Church of the Incarnation*	1969–70	All Aisle windows
BAY SHORE	*St. Peter's Church*	1965	2-light Chancel
COLUMBUS	*Trinity Episc. Church*	1968–70	All windows
ATLANTA	*St. Philip's Cathedral*	1970	Two single-lights
ASBURY PARK	*Trinity Church*	1965	3-light window Chancel
		1965	7-light West window
CHARLOTTE	*Providence Meth. Church*	1965	East window
DEARBORN	*Methodist Church*	1966–70	All windows
DALTON	*St. Agnes' Cath. Church*	1963	All windows
DETROIT	*Christian Episc. Church*	1964	3-light Sacristy
ENID	*St. Matthew's Church*	1971	Rose and Aisle windows
JANESVILLE	*St. Paul's Church*	1955	Rose window
GLEN RIDGE	*Congregational Church*	1964–65	Two 3-light Transome windows
HARTFORD	*Greek Church*	1964–65	Four single-lights
HILLSBORO	*St. Matthew's Church*	1966	Two single-lights
HICKORY	*Church of the Ascension*	1967–71	All Aisle windows
LANSING	*St. Paul's Episc. Church*	1963	7-light West window
MILFORD	*Christ Episc. Church*	1965	2-light Aisle window
NEW ORLEANS	*St. Anna's Church*	1954	East window
			West window and Aisles
NAVESINK	*All Saints' Memorial Church*	1968	Single-light window
PONCA CITY	*Grace Episcopal Church*	1965–70	All Clerestory windows
RICHMOND	*Northminster Baptist Church*	1964	All windows
	Reveille Methodist Church	1964	Circular window
RADFORD	*First Baptist Church*	1964	Single-light East window
RALEIGH	*Hayes Barton Methodist Church*	1963–64	Eight single-light windows
RUXTON	*Church of the Good Shepherd*	1964	3-light window
ROCK ISLAND	*Trinity Episcopal Church*	1966	East window
ROCK HILL	*Church of our Saviour*	1966	3-light window
RIDGEWOOD	*Christ Episcopal Church*	1966	Chancel window
RIDGEFIELD	*Zio Evang. Church*	1964	Twelve Aisle windows
			One Circular window
RIDGEWOOD	*Emmanuel Baptist Church*	1968	East window
SARANAC LAKE	*St. Luke's Church*	1965	Single-light Aisle window
SEWANEE	*University of the South*	1965–68	Three 3-light Clerestory window
STAUNTON	*St. John's Methodist Church*	1964	3-light Transept window
		1965	3-light Transept window
SCRANTON	*St. Luke's Church*	1963–65	Four 3-light Aisle windows
SULLIVANS ISLAND	*Church of the Holy Cross*	1964	Single-light Aisle window
SPRINGHILL	*St. Paul's Church*	1964	Single-light East window
SHREVEPORT	*First Baptist Church*	1963	5-light Chapel window
SUMMIT	*Christ Episcopal Church*	1964	Two single windows
SAINT JOSEPH	*Christ Episcopal Church*	1970	Single-light Aisle window
SHARON	*Rumanian Orthodox Church*	1970	Ten Aisle windows
TEANECK	*St. Paul's Lutheran Church*	1963	All windows
TULSA	*Trinity Episcopal Church*	1964–70	Crypt Chapel window
			Ten 2-light Clerestory windows
TUSCALOOSA	*Christ Episcopal Church*	1965	Two single-light Aisle windows

U.S.A. (continued)

UPPER MONTCLAIR	*Union Congregational Church*	1964	All windows
WOODLANDS	*St. Luke's Episcopal Church*	1966–70	Five 3-light windows
YONKERS	*St. Andrew's Episcopal Church*	1968	3-light window

Above and below
Trinity Church, Tulsa,
Oklahoma, U.S.A.

Three sections from one of ten
clerestory windows *(left)*
and window in Crypt Chapel
(below)

Above
St. Christopher's Church, Hinchley Wood, Surrey.

Left
St. Luke's Church, Milnsbridge, Yorkshire.

23

TRENA M. COX, FMGP
96 Watergate Street, Chester
Telephone : Chester 24901

CHESHIRE

CHESTER	*St. John's*	1969	Single-light window in Porch
DARESBURY	*Parish Church*	1960	2-light window, North Aisle
FARNDON	*Farndon*	1966	2-light window, West Wall
LATCHFORD	*Christ Church*	1969	2-light window, South Wall
MOULTON	*Parish Church*	1962	Single-light window, North Wall
PRENTON	*St. Stephen's*	1963	2-light window, South Wall
		1965	Single-light window, Lady Chapel
RUNCORN	*St. John's*	1970	West window
WOODCHURCH	*Parish Church*	1964	3-light East window, North Aisle
		1965	3-light West window, North Aisle

LANCASHIRE

BILLINGE	*Parish Church*	1966	6-light window, South Wall
SKELMERSDALE	*St. Paul's*	1961	7-light window, West Wall
		1965	3-light window in Lady Chapel
		1967	2-light window, South Wall Chapel

SHROPSHIRE

SHREWSBURY	*R.C. Cathedral*	1960	Single-light window in Porch

WALES

CAERNARVONSHIRE

BEDDGELERT	*Parish Church*	1968	2-light window, North Wall

DENBIGHSHIRE

LLANTYSILIO	*Parish Church*	1971	3-light window, South Wall
WREXHAM	*R.C. Cathedral*	1969	5-light window, East Wall

FLINTSHIRE

BISTRE	*Parish Church*	1962	Single-light window, South Wall
CONNAH'S QUAY	*R.C. Church*	1971	East window
TALLARN GREEN	*Parish Church*	1970	2-light window, North Wall

KENNETH ANTHONY CROCKER, AMGP
7212 Germantown Avenue
Philadelphia
Pennsylvania, 19119
United States of America

U.S.A.

FLORIDA

PENSACOLA	*Naval Air Station Catholic Chapel*	1966	Eight Aisle windows One Sacristy window Four 'Sand-Carved' door panels
SARASOTA	*The Church of the Redeemer*	1964–66	Eight Aisle windows Four Transept windows Two 'Heraldic' Sanctuary windows Two Narthex windows

GEORGIA

BRUNSWICK	*St. Francis Xavier Church*	1966	One large Chancel window One hundred and forty-four Clerestory windows Twenty-two Narthex windows
ST. SIMON'S ISLAND	*Christ Episcopal Church*	1967	Four 2-light with tracery windows Two narthex windows

ILLINOIS

CHICAGO	*Church of the Ascension*	1966	Four 3-light windows

MAINE

HULLS COVE	*Church of Our Father*	1968	One 2-light with tracery window

MARYLAND

BALTIMORE	*Church of the Advent*	1969	3-light with tracery Chancel window 2-light with tracery Clerestory window
BEL AIR	*Emmanuel Episcopal Church*	1963	Eight 2-light Aisle windows
COLLEGE PARK	*St. Andrew's Episcopal Church*	1969–70	Twenty-four Aisle windows
HAGERSTOWN	*St. John's Episcopal Church*	1967	Five 2-light with tracery Aisle windows Two single Narthex windows
SILVER SPRING	*Grace Episcopal Church*	1963–70	Eight 2-light Aisle windows One 2-light 'Space window'
TOWSON	*Cavalry Baptist Church*	1967	One 2-light with tracery window

MICHIGAN

DETROIT	*St. Martha's Episcopal Church*	1962–68	Twenty-four single Aisle windows
	Marillac Hall	1963	Six single-light windows

MINNESOTA

DULUTH	*St. Paul's Episcopal Church*	1967	Nine Aisle windows Two Narthex windows
MINNEAPOLIS	*Lakewood Memorial Mausoleum*	1967	Three large windows with two 'Glass mosaic' panels between windows, in lounge Eighteen large alcove windows One transom window Four 'Glass mosaic' panels
	Westminster Presbyterian Church	1964	Five single-light windows

MISSISSIPPI
MERIDIAN	*Naval Air Station*	1968–70	Nine single-light Aisle windows Two 'Gold repousse' windows

NEBRASKA
OMAHA	*First Methodist Church*	1963	Three large single-light windows One large 2-light window

NEW JERSEY
HIGHTSTOWN	*First Presbyterian Church*	1970	One single-light
PITMAN	*Church of the Good Shepherd*	1966	One single-light window
PRINCETON	*Trinity Episcopal Church*	1965	Large 4-light with Tracery West window 2-light window in Unity Chapel Two single-light Narthex windows
RUMSON	*St. George by the River Episcopal Church*	1964	One 3-light window
SEA ISLE CITY	*The United Methodist Church*	1967–68	Large 3-light Chancel window Eight single-light Aisle windows Two Narthex windows
WOODBURY	*Christ Episcopal Church*	1963–70	One 2-light window One single-light Aisle window One Transom window One Rose window

NEW YORK
PELHAM	*Huguenot Memorial Church*	1966	Nine 3-light Aisle windows
RYE	*Christ Church*	1963	Three single-light windows
SYRACUSE	*Park Central Presbyterian Church*	1964	Eleven single-light windows Five 'Sand-carved' door panels
UTICA	*Westminster Presbyterian Church*	1966	One 2-light window

NORTH CAROLINA
ASHEVILLE	*Trinity Parish Episcopal Church*	1967	5-light North Transept window 5-light South Transept window Thirteen Clerestory windows
BREVARD	*St. Philip's Episcopal Church*	1967	One single-light window

OHIO
CINCINNATI	*Spring Grove Memorial Mausoleum*	1965–70	Large 5-light Chapel window Three 3-light corridor windows Eight large alcove windows 4-light Chapel window Two corridor windows Eight terrace floor windows
DAYTON	*Woodland Memorial Mausoleum*	1969	Three large light lounge windows Five corridor windows Two Columbarium windows Large 'Glass mosaic' panel

PENNSYLVANIA
CHELTENHAM	*St. Aidan's Episcopal Church*	1968	3-light with tracery window
CHESTER	*St. Paul's Episcopal Church*	1963	Twelve single-light Aisle windows
HARRISBURG	*St. Andrew's Episcopal Church*	1969–70	Twenty-one Aisle windows
HAVERTOWN	*St. Faith Episcopal Church*	1967	Forty 2-light Chancel windows
ITHAN	*Christ Episcopal Church*	1963	Three single-light Aisle windows 4-light West window

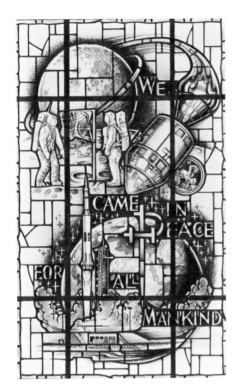

Above
Spring Grove Memorial Mausoleum, Cincinnati, Ohio, U.S.A.

Apollo 11 Moon Landing — July 20th 1969 *(left)* and Peaceful use of the atom *(right)*

Left
First Presbyterian Church, Hightstown, New Jersey, U.S.A.

'Parsifal' — Woodland Mausoleum, Dayton, Ohio, U.S.A.

PENNSYLVANIA (continued)

PARKSBURG	*Upper Octorara Presbyterian Church*	1965	Two 2-light windows
PHILADELPHIA	*St. Martin's in the Field Episcopal Church Chestnut Hill*	1962	Three 2-light Aisle windows
KENSINGTON	*St. Paul's Episcopal Church*	1965	One single-light Chancel window
ROXBOROUGH	*St. Timothy's Episcopal Church*	1963–69	Two transom windows Two dormer windows One side Chancel window
PITTSBURGH	*Mount Lebanon Methodist Church*	1964	Two 3-light Praise and Prayer windows Large 5-light Parable window
		1964	Ten panel Narthex screen
WALLINGFORD	*Wallingford Presbyterian Church*	1970	3-light with tracery West window
WAYNE	*St. Mary's Episcopal Church*	1970	Four Chancel windows Four single Aisle windows Two quadrafoil Transept windows

SOUTH CAROLINA

CHERAW	*St. David's Episcopal Church*	1967	Three single-light windows

VIRGINIA

HARRISONBURG	*Emmanuel Episcopal Church*	1962	Eight 2-light Aisle windows Two Narthex windows
RICHMOND	*All Saints' Episcopal Church*	1966	5-light window
STANTON	*St. Faith Lutheran Church*	1962–66	Six single colonial Aisle windows

WASHINGTON

EVERETT	*First Presbyterian Church*	1969	5-light corridor window
KENT	*St. James' Episcopal Church*	1964	Eight single-light Aisle windows

WEST VIRGINIA

HUNTINGDON	*Trinity Episcopal Church*	1966	Seven single-light Aisle windows

ADDENDUM

Developed designs while an employee of the Willet Stained Glass Studios, within their plans and specifications, under their supervision for windows created by the Willet Studios in the foregoing churches.

CAMBRIDGESHIRE

CAMBRIDGE	*Trinity College*	1956	Two heraldic panels

CHESHIRE

APPLETON THORN	*Holy Cross*	1970	East window (in progress)
BOSLEY	*St. Mary the Virgin*	1967–68	East window and two single windows, North Aisle

DURHAM Co.

SOUTH SHIELDS	*St. Hilda*	1952	Three windows in Apse

HUNTINGDONSHIRE

HOUGHTON	*St. Mary the Virgin*	1959	2-light window, North Aisle

LANCASHIRE

ALDINGHAM	*St. Cuthbert*	1964	East window
ASPULL	*St. Elizabeth*	1954–66	Two lights, North and South Aisles
BIRKDALE	*St. James'*	1965	3-light window, North Transept
BLACKBURN	*St. Philip, Witton*	1950	Single-light window, North Aisle
BLACKPOOL	*St. Paul, Marton*	1950	3-light window, North Aisle
BOOTLE	*Christ Church*	1953	Single-light window, Lady Chapel
CHATBURN	*Christ Church*	1949	Single-light window, North Wall
GRESSINGHAM	*St. John*	1958	2-light window, Baptistery
HABERGHAM	*All Saints'*	1960	2-light window, Baptistery
LEIGH	*St. John the Evangelist*	1969	3-light window, South Aisle
LITTLE HULTON	*St. Paul, Peel*	1968	2-light window, North Aisle
LIVERPOOL	*Parish Church*	1951	3-light window, South Aisle
	St. Simon and St. Jude	1947	Single-light window, South Aisle
MANCHESTER	*St. Michael, Peel Green*	1957	East window
OLDHAM	*St. Andrew*	1969	Two single-light windows, West Wall
READ-IN-WHALLEY	*St. John*	1949	2-light window, North Aisle
ROCHDALE	*St. Anne's, Belfield*	1956	East window
SCARISBRICK	*St. Mark's*	1955	2-light window, South Aisle
		1965	Single-light window, South Aisle
SOUTHPORT	*St. Paul's*	1953	Three 2-light windows, North Aisle
WESHAM	*Christ Church*	1948	2-light window, North Aisle
WHELLEY	*St. Stephen's*	1959	Four lights, Baptistery
WIDNES	*St. Paul's*	1959–64	Four single-light windows, North and South Aisles

MIDDLESEX

FINCHLEY	*St. Mary's*	1953–54	East windows of Chancel and Chapel

NORFOLK

THETFORD	*St. Cuthbert's*	1962	2-light window, South Aisle

STAFFORDSHIRE

CHEBSEY	*All Saints'*	1950	2-light window, North Aisle
HAUGHTON	*St. Giles'*	1946	Single-light window, North Wall

SUFFOLK

SANTON DOWNHAM	*St. Mary the Virgin*	1953	Single-light Chancel window

YORKSHIRE

BARNOLDSWICK	*Parish Church*	1960	Single-light window, South Transept

BEMPTON	*St. Michael's*	1962	2-light window, North Aisle
BRADFORD	*St. John's, Great Horton*	1960	Three windows in Apse
FEATHERSTONE	*All Saints'*	1963	2-light window, West Wall
KEYINGHAM	*St. Nicholas'*	1960	3-light window, North Aisle
LOCKWOOD	*Emmanuel*	1961	2-light window, North Aisle
MIRFIELD	*Parish Church*	1959	2-light window in Chapel
NORTON	*St. Peter's*	1963	2-light window, North Aisle
SHELLEY	*Emmanuel*	1961	Rose window
STOKESLEY	*Parish Church*	1962	Single-light window, South Aisle
WRENTHORPE	*St. Anne's*	1969	Single-light window, South Aisle
YORK	*Minster*	1949	Heraldic panel in Nave
	St. Luke's	1951–59	Three single-light windows, Lady Chapel

WALES

ANGLESEY
LLANFAES	*St. Catherine's*	1964	2-light window, South Aisle

CAERNARVONSHIRE
DEGANWY	*Woodlands School*	1956	East window of Chapel

ISLE OF MAN

RAMSEY	*St. Olave's*	1963	Two single-light windows, North Aisle and West Wall

NORTHERN IRELAND

Co. ANTRIM
BALLYMENA	*St. Patrick's*	1957	2-light windows, North and South Aisles

ABROAD

GIBRALTAR	*Cathedral*	1957	East window

St. Mary the Virgin, Bosley,
Nr. Macclesfield, Cheshire.

Above left
St. James, Birkdale, Lancashire.

Above right
St. Elizabeth, Aspull, Lancashire.

Opposite
All Saints, Habergham, Burnley, Lancashire.

33

BEDFORDSHIRE

CLIFTON	*Parish Church*	1951	5-light East window
			2-light window
LEAGRAVE	*St. Luke's*	1960	Lady Chapel window

BERKSHIRE

ABINGDON	*Parish Church*	1965	Single-light window
BISHAM	*Parish Church*	1970	Single-light window (St. Clare)
ENGLEFIELD GREEN	*Parish Church*	1966	2-light window
SHIPPON	*Parish Church*	1964–70	Two 2-light windows
TILEHURST	*Parish Church*	1965–70	6-light East window
WARFIELD	*Parish Church*	1960	East window Lady Chapel

BUCKINGHAMSHIRE

ASTON SANDFORD	*Parish Church*	1969	2-light window
BUCKINGHAM	*Parish Church*	1967	Two single-light windows
HADDENHAM	*Parish Church*	1949	3-light window
		1953	Two trefoil windows
LITTLE HAMPDEN	*Parish Church*	1951	West window
			Two 2-light windows
LITTLE HORWOOD	*Parish Church*	1955	East window
PRESTWOOD	*Parish Church*	1969	West window
			Single-light Lady Chapel window
SOULBURY	*Parish Church*	1956	3-light window (St. Michael)

CAMBRIDGESHIRE

THRIPLOW	*Parish Church*	1971	Single-light window (St. Catherine)

DEVONSHIRE

EXETER	*Cathedral*	1951	Great West window
		1947	Devon Regiment Memorial
EXFORD	*Parish Church*	1938	Two 3-light windows

DORSET

MILTON ABBAS	*Parish Church*	1971	3-light window
STOKE ABBOTT	*Parish Church*	1957	Single-light Chancel window

ESSEX

PANFIELD	*Parish Church*	1956	East window
STOCK	*Parish Church*	1950–59	All windows

HAMPSHIRE

BEAULIEU	*Abbey*	1948	Single-light window (St. Francis)
PORTSDOWN	*Parish Church*	1947	2nd Army Memorial
		1955–63	Ten 2-light windows
PORTSMOUTH	*Royal Garrison Church*	1966–70	Three 3-light windows
SOUTHAMPTON	*St. Jude's*	1962	Single-light window

KENT

ASHFORD	*Wye College Chapel*	1950	West window
CANTERBURY	*Kent County Hospital*	1937	Children's Ward
SHORNECLIFFE	*Garrison Church*	1959–65	Two single-light windows
SITTINGBOURNE	*Parish Church*	1953	3-light window (Heraldry)

LEICESTERSHIRE

LEICESTER	*Chest Hospital*	1961	3-light window (Nativity)
	St. Augustine's Church	1967	East window (Left and Right lights)

LINCOLNSHIRE

METHERINGHAM	*Parish Church*	1968	3-light window South side

LONDON

	All Hallows by the Tower	1948–66	All windows
	Middlesex Hospital Chapel	1948–52	All windows
	Ironmongers Hall	1948–53	All windows
ALDERSGATE	*St. Botolph's*	1955–58	Four windows
CROWN COURT (DRURY LANE)	*Church of Scotland*	1947–70	All windows
LEADENHALL STREET	*St. Catherine Cree*	1963	'Lancastria' Memorial
ROTHERHITHE	*St. Crispin with Christ Church*	1963	5-light window
DULWICH	*James Allen's Girl's School*	1969	Gustav Holst Memorial

MIDDLESEX

HARROW SCHOOL	*War Memorial*	1958	All windows

MONMOUTHSHIRE

MOUNTON (CHEPSTOW)		1961	2-light window

NORFOLK

NARBOROUGH	*Parish Church*	1950	Three 3-light windows
QUIDENHAM	*Parish Church*	1945	9th U.S. Army Air Force Memorial

NORTHAMPTONSHIRE

EASTON NESTON	*Parish Church*	1968	3-light Chancel window
PETERBOROUGH	*Christ-the-Carpenter*	1970	East window

NOTTINGHAMSHIRE

SANDIACRE	*Parish Church*	1956	Single-light window South side

OXFORDSHIRE

BEGBROKE	*Parish Church*	1956	East window
CHARLTON-ON-OTMOOR	*Parish Church*	1969	Two 2-light windows (Heraldry)

SOMERSET

BATH	*Abbey*	1955	Great East window
	Magdalen Chapel	1954	East window
	St. Barnabas (Southdown)	1958	East window
	Royal National Hospital for Rheumatic Diseases	1959–61	Four 3-light windows
		1965	7-light East window

SUFFOLK

EASTON	*Parish Church*	1965	2-light window

SURREY

PURLEY	*R. Russell Schools*	1938–64	All windows

SUSSEX

BRIGHTON	*Roedean School*	1960	Royal Arms
EASTBOURNE	*St. Andrew's Presbyterian Church*	1963	Single-light window

WARWICKSHIRE

Coventry	*St. Mary's Hall*	1947	All windows

Right
Parish Church, Bisham, Berkshire.

Left
Parish Church, Metheringham, Lincolnshire.

36

YORKSHIRE
YORK

York Minster   1947   K.O.Y.L.I. Memorial window

ISLE OF WIGHT

MOTTISTONE   1950   East window
                                                Lady Chapel window

NORTHERN IRELAND

DERRY Co.
KILLALOO   *Parish Church*   1966   Two 2-light windows

ABROAD

CANADA
LIVERPOOL N.S.   *Holy Trinity*   1958   Two single-light windows
BRANTFORD,   *H.M's. Chapel Royal*   1961   Eight single-light windows
ONTARIO   *of the Mohawks*
LONDON, ONTARIO   *Bishop Cronyn*   1965   All windows
                        Memorial Chapel
GRAND BEND   *St. John's by the Lake* 1966   Single-light window

NEW ZEALAND
MOUNT SOMERS   *Parish Church*   1953   Single-light window

NIGERIA
AKURE   *Fiwasaiye Girls School* 1968   3-light window
                        Chapel
LAGOS   *Mr. Fawehinini's House* 1966   Single-light window

TANZANIA
ARUSHA   *Christ Church*   1965–69   Four single-light windows

ROGER FIFIELD, ATD, AMGP
Attleborough Vicarage, Nuneaton, Warwickshire

NORTHAMPTONSHIRE
BOUGHTON   1968   Two heraldic windows in a
                                           private house

SOMERSET
CONGRESBURY   1971   3-light West window in South
                                           Aisle

WARWICKSHIRE
BEDWORTH   1966   3-light West window in Nave

Parish Church, Bedworth, Warwickshire.

CHARLES W. FLORENCE, DA, AMGP
61 East Church Street, Buckie, Banffshire, Scotland

SCOTLAND

BANFFSHIRE

GLENLIVET	*Archbreck Church*	1956	Circular window Last Supper
		1958	Circular window annunciation
		1964	Lancet window Harvest Thanksgiving
		1964	Lancet window Industries of Banffshire
		1965	Lancet window Gethsemane
		1966	Lancet window Pieta
		1968	Lancet window Resurrection
		1969	Lancet window Emmaus
DUFFTOWN	*St. Michael's Church*	1971	Lancet window St. Michael

MORAYSHIRE

LOSSIEMOUTH	*St. James's Church*	1971	5-light window The Miraculous Catch

BERKSHIRE

ETON	*College Chapel*	1954–59	Armorial windows in Nave, four North, four South

DEVONSHIRE

BRIXHAM	*Catholic Church*	1966	Window in Blessed Sacrament Chapel
	British Seamen's Boys' Home	1968	West window
TIVERTON	*Bickley Church*	1941	Carew Memorial window

HAMPSHIRE

FORDINGBRIDGE	*Breamore Church*	1935	St. Christopher window
ROMSEY	*Awbridge Church*	1955	Fetherstonhaugh Memorial window
WINCHESTER	*Twyford Church*	1965	West window

KENT

CHELSFIELD	*Parish Church*	1948	East window
			St. John's Chapel windows
CHEVENING	*Parish Church*	1948	Stanhope Chantry windows
		1950	East window
HIGHAM	*St. John's Church*	1954	East window
		1957	Two Chancel windows
SNODLAND	*Parish Church*	1966	Pilgrims' window (Dedrick Memorial)

LANCASHIRE

ASHTON-UNDER-LYNE	*Parish Church*	1964	Wilson Memorial window

LONDON

CITY	*St. Paul's Cathedral*	1968	St. Christopher, Crypt Chapel (Glass appliqué)
SW1	*St. Columba's, Church of Scotland*	1955	East (Rose) window
			Regimental Chapel window
TEMPLE	*Middle Temple*	1949	Lord Chancellors' window
			Drake Lantern
CLAPHAM	*Grafton Square Congregational Church*	1958	West window
DULWICH	*St. Stephen's Church, Sydenham Hill*	1952	West window
WOOD GREEN	*St. Paul's Church*	1970	Sanctuary windows
			Regina Cæli window (Glass appliqué)

NORFOLK

FAKENHAM	*Tatterford Church*	1953	East window
HOLBEACH HURN	*Parish Church*	1947	West window
		1949	St. Michael, St. Christopher windows
NORWICH	*Cathedral*	1963	Benedictine window

SURREY

FARNHAM	*St. Thomas-on-the-Bourne*	1956	Julian of Norwich window
	Heath End, Catholic Church	1960	East window
		1969	Holy Family window
			Baptism window
		1971	Resurrection window

GUILDFORD	*Cathedral*	1940	East (Rose) window
		1952	Children's window
			High Sheriffs' window
		1957	W.R.A.C. window
		1959	Doctors' window
		1962	Building Craft Livery Companies' window
	St. Martha's-on-the-Hill	1953	East window

SUSSEX

FRISTON	*St. James's Church*	1952	Stutchbury Memorial
WILLINGDON	*St. Mary's-in-the-Park*	1953	East window

WARWICKSHIRE

BIRMINGHAM	*King Edward's Grammar School*	1947	Founder's window

YORKSHIRE

BRADFORD	*Cathedral*	1956	
		1968	Song Room windows
		1969	Hodgson Memorial

SCILLY ISLES

ST. AGNES	*Parish Church*	1967	East window

'Regina Caeli' —
St. Paul's Church,
Wood Green, London.

Right
Eton College Chapel, Berkshire.
Godolphin Arms.

Left
Norwich Cathedral. Detail from
Benedictine Window — Gregory the
Great sending St. Augustine to
England.

DONALD C. GELDER
R.O.3. Attica, New York, 14011, U.S.A.

ABROAD

U.S.A.
  NEW YORK   *St. Stephen's Episcopal*   Two Nave windows
                            Church, Niagara Falls

Above
St. Stephen's Episcopal Church, Niagara Falls, New York, U.S.A.

Detail of Resurrection Window — Modern family at grace *(left)*.
Detail of Teaching Window — Sunday School class *(right)*.

L. P. GINEVER
45 Station Road, Sutton in Ashfield, Notts.

NOTTINGHAM
BULWELL   *St. Mary's*   1951   2-light window

St. Mary's, Bulwell, Nottingham.

GODDARD & GIBBS STUDIOS
A. E. Buss, FMGP; J. N. Lawson, AMGP
41/49 Kingsland Road, Shoreditch E2 8AD

BEDFORDSHIRE

HENLOW	*RAF Chapel*	1967	Single-light window
LUTON	*St. Andrew's*	1969	Two 4-light windows
		1970	3-light window
RENHOLD	*All Saints'*	1966	3-light window
YELDON	*St. Mary's*	1966	3-light window

BERKSHIRE

DRAYTON	*St. Peter's*	1965	Single-light window
SUNNINGHILL	*St. Michael and All Angels*	1969	Two 2-light windows

BUCKINGHAMSHIRE

HIGH WYCOMBE	*Hazlemere Parish*	1963	Two 3-light windows
NEWPORT PAGNELL	*St. Luke's*	1963–68	Two single-light windows
			East window
			Circular West window
WOOBURN	*St. Paul's*	1961	3-light window

CHESHIRE

BIRKENHEAD	*St. Saviour's*	1968	Single-light window
CHESTER		1965	3-light window
ELLESMERE PORT	*St. Thomas'*	1969	Two 3-light windows
WHARTON	*Christ Church*	1968	2-light window

DEVONSHIRE

CHAGFORD		1969	3-light window
SATTERLEIGH	*St. Peter's*	1965	3-light window

DORSET

POOLE	*St. John's*	1965	Single-light window

DURHAM Co.

WEST HARTLEPOOL	*St. Paul's*	1965	Single-light window

ESSEX

CHADWELL HEATH	*St. Chad's*	1966	Single-light window
CHIGWELL	*St. Mary's*	1962	2-light window
	St. Winifred's	1963	Single-light window
DAGENHAM	*The Holy Family*	1967	Single-light window
HALSTEAD	*St. Francis of Assisi R.C.*	1970	Single-light window
LEIGH-ON-SEA	*R.C. Our Lady of Lourdes*	1962	Single-light window
		1964	3-light window
	Methodist Church	1965	Single-light window
LITTLE THURROCK	*St. Mary's*	1966	3-light window
THORPE BAY	*Methodist Church*	1960–70	Seven single-light windows
UPMINSTER	*Methodist*	1963	Two 3-light windows

HAMPSHIRE

SOUTHSEA	*St. Margaret's*		3-light window
			Single-light window
WINCHESTER	*St. Peter's*		Two 3-light windows

HEREFORDSHIRE

PETERCHURCH	*St. Peter's*	1970	2-light window

HERTFORDSHIRE

LEMSFORD	St. Mary's (Brocket Chapel)	1968	3-light window
LETCHWORTH	St. Thomas of Canterbury	1968	Single-light window
ST. ALBANS	St. Stephen's	1965	2-light window
WARE	Sacred Heart and St. Joseph R.C.	1970	2-light window East window

KENT

DEAL	St. Michael and All Angels R.C.	1965	Single-light window
MINSTER-IN-SHEPPEY	Abbey	1965	Single-light window
RAMSGATE	St. George's	1961	6-light East window 2-light Warrior's Chapel window
SELLING	St. Mary's	1970	2-light window
SHEPPEY	Minster Abbey	1964	Single-light window
		1965	3-light West window Single-light window
SYDENHAM	Church of Our Lady and Phillip Neri	1965	3-light window

LINCOLNSHIRE

SPALDING	St. John's	1966–70	Three single-light windows

LONDON

ACTON	Baptist Church	1962	Single-light window
	St. Martin's	1967	Three single-light windows
ALDGATE	St. Botolph's	1969–70	Four single-light windows
CRIPPLEGATE	St. Giles'	1968	5-light West window
EAST HAM	St. George's	1961	5-light window
FINCHLEY	St. Mary's	1966	2-light window
GOLDERS GREEN	St. Edward the Confessor	1968	3-light window
GUILDHALL	East Crypt	1971	Six 3-light windows
HERNE HILL	St. Jude's	1964	Single-light window
HOMERTON	St. Domonic's	1962	Fifteen single-light windows
LOTHBURY EC2	St. Margaret's	1963	Single-light window
		1969	Single-light window
MUSWELL HILL	St. Andrew's	1967	Single-light window
	St. Peter-le-Poer	1969	2-light window
MYDDLETON SQUARE	St. Mark's	1962	3-light East window
PALMERS GREEN	St. John's	1962	Two 3-light windows
ROTHERHITHE	Norwegian Seamen's Mission	1968	Four single-light windows
SOUTHAMPTON ROW	St. Domonic's Priory	1962	2-light window
TOTTENHAM	Methodist Church	1964	Four single-light windows
WEST EALING	St. John's	1970	2-light window
WIMBLEDON	Trinity Presbyterian Church	1969	Three single-light windows

MIDDLESEX

ENFIELD	St. John's, Clayhill	1970	2-light window
HARMONDSWORTH	St. Mary's	1968	2-light window
HAYES	New Catholic Church	1961	Thirty panels in East End and Sanctuary
	St. Anselm's	1964	3-light window
HILLINGDON	St. Andrew's	1963	4-light window

MONMOUTHSHIRE

DEGAWNAY	All Saints'	1963	2-light window
WHITSON	Parish Church	1962	Single-light window

NOTTINGHAMSHIRE

HUTHWAITE	*All Saints'*	1964	3-light window
		1966	3-light window
KIRKBY-IN-ASHFIELD	*St. Wilfred's*	1965	2-light window

STAFFORDSHIRE

BARTON-UNDER-NEEDWOOD	*St. James'*	1970	3-light window
BLITHFIELD	*St. Leonard's*	1965	Two 2-light windows
			5-light window
BRIERLEY HILL	*St. John's Brockmoor*	1965	Single-light window
BUTHFIELD	*St. Leonard's*	1964	2-light window
STAFFORD	*St. Mary's Castle Church*	1964	Single-light window
SUTTON BONNINGTON	*St. Michael's*	1963	2-light window
			3-light window
UTTOXETER	*St. Lawrence's, Bramshall*	1964	3-light East window
WALSALL	*St. Matthew's*	1962	One 3-light window

SUFFOLK

BEYTON	*All Saints'*	1970	2-light window
IPSWICH	*Congregational Church*	1966	4-light window

SURREY

CHOBHAM	*St. Lawrence*	1961	3-light East window
CROYDON	*Congregational*	1964	West window
	St. George's, Shirley	1970	Single-light window
FRIMLEY	*Catholic Church*	1969	Two 3-light windows
NEW MALDEN	*Christ Church*	1964	2-light window
WINDLESHAM	*Hall Inn*	1965	9-light window

SUSSEX

BURGESS HILL	*St. George's Convent*	1968	2-light window
CROWBOROUGH	*Outward Bound School*	1964	All windows
LANCING	*College*	1961	Single-light window
NINFIELD	*St. Mary's*	1961	2-light window

WARWICKSHIRE

COVENTRY	*St. Thomas's*	1964	2-light window
STRATFORD-ON-AVON	*Methodist Church (Sandblast)*	1964	4-light window
			Two doors

WESTMORLAND

LUPTON	*St. John's*	1970	Single-light window

WILTSHIRE

RUSHALL	*St. Matthew's*	1968	2-light window

WORCESTERSHIRE

BEWDLEY	*St. Giles'*	1964	3-light window
HEIGHTLINGTON			
KIDDERMINSTER	*Holy Trinity, Far Forest*	1962	Five single-light windows
		1965	2-light window

YORKSHIRE

BARNSLEY	*St. Peter's*	1963	Tracery window
HARROGATE	*College Chapel*	1963	4-light West window
			3-light East window
REDCAR	*Church of St. William Dormanstown*	1964	Two single-light windows

WALES

CAERNARVONSHIRE
LLANDUDNO	*St. Paul's*	1965	2-light window
LLANGWSTENIN	*St. Michael's*	1966	5-light window

DENBIGHSHIRE
PONTFADOG	*St. John the Baptist*	1967	3-light window
			Single-light window

FLINTSHIRE
LLANFERRES	*St. Berris*	1966	3-light window
RHYL	*St. John the Baptist*	1963	Single-light window
		1970	5-light East window
WHITFORD	*St. Beuno and St. Mary*	1968	2-light window

ABROAD

AUSTRALIA
ADELAIDE	*St. Oswald's Church*	1963	Single-light window

BERMUDA
HAMILTON	*Holy Trinity*	1965–68	Four single-light windows

CANADA
BRITISH COLUMBIA
VICTORIA	*Veterans' Hospital*	1962	Three single-light windows
	St. Matthias'	1965	3-light Baptistery window
		1970	Two single-light windows

ONTARIO
WESTON	*Westminster United*	1962	2-light window
	Church	1969–70	2-light window
			Single-light window

NEW ZEALAND
AWAPUNI	*Parish Church*	1962	Single-light window
PALMERSTONE N.	*St. Paul's Methodist*	1963	2-light window

SOUTH AFRICA
DURBAN	*St. John the Divine*	1962	3-light window
	Church	1965	Rose window
JOHANNESBURG	*St. Andrew's, Kensington*	1964	Three single-light windows
		1969–70	4-light window
			2-light window
PRETORIA	*St. Alban's Cathedral*	1968	Single-light window

TUNISIA
TUNIS	*St. George's*	1964	3-light East window

U.S.A.
CONNECTICUT	*St. James's Episcopal*	1962	2-light window

WEST INDIES
JAMAICA	*St. Elizabeth's*	1970	Single-light window
NASSAU, BAHAMAS	*St. Andrew's*	1966	Single-light window

WINDOWS IN GLASS AND CONCRETE/EPOXY RESIN

BERKSHIRE
HARMAN'S WATER	*Bracknell New Church*	1970	One window

BUCKINGHAMSHIRE
LONG CRENDON	*New Catholic Church*	1970	Twenty-four windows

KENT			
SPELDHURST	*College of Psycho-Therapeutics*	1969	One large window

LONDON			
BARKING	*Hospital Chapel*	1968	One large window
MILLWALL	*St. Luke's Church*	1961	Three windows
ST. JOHN'S WOOD	*Convent Chapel*	1964	Four windows

MIDDLESEX			
PERIVALE	*St. John Fisher Church*	1970	Ten windows

SUSSEX			
CRAWLEY	*St. Alban's Church*	1961	Five windows
LODSWORTH	*Parish Church*	1968	One window

WORCESTERSHIRE			
WORCESTER	*New Methodist Church*	1968	Large Staircase window

EIRE

KILLINEY	*Convent of the Holy Child*	1961	Twelve windows

ABROAD

BAHREIN	*New Secretariat Building*	1968	Large staircase window

The Guildhall, London. One of a set of six windows.
Designed by Arthur Buss.

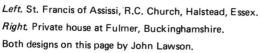

Left. St. Francis of Assissi, R.C. Church, Halstead, Essex.

Right. Private house at Fulmer, Buckinghamshire.

Both designs on this page by John Lawson.

50

Above
Part of window at Christ Church, Staines, Middlesex.

Right
Lodsworth Parish Church, Sussex. Depicting St. Nicholas.

Below
The Casino, Gibraltar.

All designs on this page by Arthur Buss.

51

DEVONSHIRE
EXETER — *Cathedral* — 1953 — Window in East wall of Lady Chapel

DORSET
CHURCH KNOWLE — *St. Peter's* — 1955 — 2-light window in North wall of Nave
2-light window in East wall of South Transept

DURHAM CO.
SUNDERLAND — *St. Gabriel's* — 1953 — Window in East wall of Memorial Chapel

ESSEX
NORTH FAMBRIDGE — *Holy Trinity* — 1964 — East window
SPRINGFIELD — *All Saints'* — 1961 — 3-light window in South wall of Nave
3-light window in North wall of Nave

HUNTINGDONSHIRE
HOUGHTON — *St. Mary's* — 1959 — 2-light window in South Wall of Chancel

LINCOLNSHIRE
LINCOLN — *Training College Chapel* — 1960 — Single lancet in South Wall of Nave

LONDON
CLAPHAM COMMON — *Holy Trinity* — 1957 — 3-light window in South Wall of Lady Chapel

SOMERSET
BLEADON — *St. Peter's and St. Paul's* — 1964 — East window
CREWKERNE — *St. Bartholomew's* — 1963 — 3-light East window of North Transept
CHARD — *St. John's* — 1968 — 2-light window in South Chancel

YORKSHIRE
ROMALDKIRK — *St. Romand's* — 1960 — 3-light window in South wall of Sanctuary

ABROAD

CANADA
WESTHOLME, VANCOUVER ISLAND — *All Saints'* — 1957 — East window

SOUTH AFRICA
FORT BEAUFORT — *St. John Baptist* — 1959 — East window

Opposite
Church of St. Peter and St. Paul, Bleadon, Somerset.

53

JOHN HARDMAN STUDIOS
Lightwoods Park, Hagley Road West, Worley, Worcestershire
Telephone : 021–429–7609

BERKSHIRE

DOUAI ABBEY	*Abbot's Chapel*	1966	6 lights abstract coloured glazing

CAMBRIDGESHIRE

ELY	*St. Etheldreda's*	1958–70	Three 2-lights Nave windows
WIMBLINGTON	*Parish Church*	1962–63	Two 2-light windows in South Wall

CHESHIRE

CHESTER	*Pepper Street*	1965	Precinct Screen slab in concrete
WINSFORD	*White Lion Hotel*	1964	Two panels – slab in concrete

CUMBERLAND

CARLISLE	*St. Bede's*	1965	Baptistery window
KELLS	*St. Mary's*	1961	Baptistery window

DERBYSHIRE

DERBY	*Queens Hall Methodist*	1965	Circular West window
	Royal Infirmary	1961	Chapel window
	St. Alkmund	1971	Seven windows – slab in resin

DEVONSHIRE

CHELSTON	*Holy Angels*	1962	4-light Sanctuary and Nave windows

DORSET

WEYMOUTH	*St. Augustine's*	1971	Single-light South Wall window

DURHAM CO.

STANLEY	*St. Joseph's*	1959–66	3 lights window in Nave
WEST HARTLEPOOL	*St. Paul's*	1968	One single-light and Rose window West Wall

ESSEX

BEAUMONT	*Parish Church*	1961	2-light South Aisle window
ILFORD	*St. Andrew's*	1965–66	Two 2-light South Chancel windows
WESTCLIFFE	*St. Helen's*	1952–63	Six windows East Wall, South Aisle and Baptistery

GLOUCESTERSHIRE

DOWN HATHERLEY	*Parish Church*	1967	2-light window in South Wall
HASELTON	*Parish Church*	1966	2-light window in North Wall
NYMPSFIELD	*Marist Convent*	1966	Three windows – slab in concrete

HAMPSHIRE

LISS	*Le Court Home*	1961	4 lights windows in Chapel
WESTBOURNE	*Immaculate Conception*	1961–62	19 lights Nave and Chapel window

HEREFORDSHIRE

CAYNHAM	*Parish Church*	1962	Single-light South Chancel window
DONNINGTON	*Parish Church*	1969	2-light North Nave window
FELTON	*Parish Church*	1961	2-light North Wall window
ULLINGSWICK	*Parish Church*	1963	2-light South Nave window
YARKHILL	*Parish Church*	1964	3-light East window

HERTFORDSHIRE

REDBOURN	*St. John Fisher*	1966	Nave and Baptistery – slab in resin

KENT

BECKENHAM	*St. Edmund's*	1971	Two Nave windows
CHISLEHURST	*St. Mary's*	1970	2-light window in South Nave
PETTS WOOD	*St. James'*	1965–66	4 lights – slab in concrete
THANET	*Crematorium*	1966	5-light – slab in concrete

LANCASHIRE

CARNFORTH	*Our Lady's*	1967	4-light window in Baptistery
LIVERPOOL	*R.C. Cathedral*	1967	Abstract coloured glazing St. Thomas Aquinas Chapel
	City Museum	1967	Twenty-three windows – slab in concrete
MAGHULL	*St. George's*	1970	Glazed Sanctuary Screen
STONYHURST	*College*	1950–66	Heraldic Panels
WEST DERBY	*Broughton Hall*	1961–62	12 lights window in Chapel

LEICESTERSHIRE

COALVILLE	*St. Wilfrid's*	1967	5 lights windows Lady Chapel and Baptistery
FLECKNEY	*Parish Church*	1968	2-light East window of South Aisle
LOUGHBOROUGH	*St. Mary's*	1960	3 lights window in Nave
WHITWICK	*Holy Cross*	1948–64	Five 3-light Chapel windows 4 lights windows in Nave and Baptistery

LONDON

CROMWELL ROAD	*International Hotel*	1970	Globe feature slab in resin
GRAFTON STREET	*Bank of Australia and New Zealand*	1967	Entrance panel – slab in resin
HAMPSTEAD	*Netherhall House*	1966	Chapel Windows etc. – slab in resin
LONDON DOCKS	*St. Peter's*	1962–71	3 lights window in South Wall
PADDINGTON	*Technical College*	1968	Screen in appliqué
RUSSELL SQUARE	*Bloomsbury Centre Hotel*	1969	Various panels – slab in resin
STEPNEY	*St. Boniface*	1970	Two windows – slab in concrete and resin
WELBECK STREET	*Clifton Ford Hotel*	1964–69	Screens and doors – appliqué

MIDDLESEX

PONDERS END	*St. Mary's*	1959–61	Five windows in Sanctuary

NORTHAMPTONSHIRE

BRADDEN	*Parish Church*	1961	West window of South Aisle
NORTHAMPTON	*R.C. Cathedral*	1958–61	3-light East window (old glass adapted) 4 lights windows in Chapel and Baptistery

NORTHUMBERLAND

NEWCASTLE	*Holy Name*	1963	Single-light window in Nave
WALLSEND	*St. Columba's*	1960	2 lights in Chapel and Baptistery

NOTTINGHAMSHIRE

ARNOLD	*Methodist Church*	1968	East window – slab in resin
MANTON	*St. Paul's Church*	1968	Seven windows – slab in resin
OLD BASFORD	*Methodist Church*	1969	19 lights abstract coloured glazing

SHROPSHIRE

NASH	*Parish Church*	1968	2-light window in North Aisle
WROCKWARDINE	*Parish Church*	1962	2-light window West of North Aisle

SOMERSET

FROME	*Parish Church*	1962	Single-light South Aisle window
WESTON-SUPER-MARE	*Corpus Christi*	1970–71	4 lights window in Nave

STAFFORDSHIRE

ALDRIDGE	*St. Francis School*	1969	Two windows – slab in resin
CALDMORE	*St. Michael's*	1966	3 lights window in East Wall
CHASETOWN	*St. Joseph's*	1961	10 lights window and East Rose
FOREBRIDGE	*Parish Church*	1962	4-light South Transept window
HEDNESFORD	*Our Lady's*	1962–68	4-light Santuary window
			2-light Baptistery window
LOWER GORNAL	*Parish Church*	1967	2-light window in West Wall
	St. Peter's	1967	Four windows – slab in resin
MARCHINGTON	*St. Thomas'*	1966	3-light Baptistery window
NEWCASTLE	*High School*	1967	Armorial window in Memorial Hall
OGLEY HAY	*Parish Church*	1964	East window
TUNSTALL	*Sacred Heart*	1967	Narthex panels engraved
WALSALL	*St. Peter's*	1961–69	Nave windows
WEDNESBURY	*Canon Bathurst School*	1966	Engraved and appliqué panel
	St. Mary's	1960–65	Three 2-light South Aisle windows
WEST BROMWICH	*Holy Trinity*	1957–64	3 lights Nave window
WOLSTANTON	*St. Wulstan's*	1969	All windows
WOLVERHAMPTON	*Jeffcote Cemetery*	1968	Single-light Chapel window
	St. Joseph's	1967	All windows

SUFFOLK

MILDENHALL	*RAF Centre Chapel*	1971	15 lights abstract coloured glazing

SURREY

KINGSTON HILL	*St. Anne's*	1960	East window
LIGHTWATER	*Parish Church*	1964	3-light West window
WEYBRIDGE	*St. George's College*	1964	Single-light Chapel window

WARWICKSHIRE

BADDESLEY CLINTON	*Manor*	1966	Four heraldic lights
BALSALL HEATH	*St. Barnabas*	1963	3-light Lady Chapel window
BIRMINGHAM	*Carrs Lane Congregational*	1969	8 lights abstract coloured glazing
	Cathedral House	1964	5-light window in corridor
	Q.E. Hospital	1961	Chapel window
	St. Catherine's	1964	Nine 3-light windows
	St. Paul's	1966	Restoration 18th century East window
	St. Vincent's	1968	All windows abstract coloured glazing
	Sandon Road Methodist	1966	2-light window in North Aisle
	Synagogue	1956–69	Thirty-nine windows
CASTLE BROMWICH	*St. Wilfrid's*	1965	All windows abstract coloured glazing
COVENTRY	*All Souls'*	1952–71	Eleven windows
	Polish Church	1963	2 lights window in East Wall
	St. Elizabeth's	1962	14 lights windows in Sanctuary and Chapels
	Stoke St. Michael	1955–60	3-light window
			Two 2-light windows
	Synagogue	1953–61	Three windows
HAMPTON-ON-THE-HILL	*St. Charles'*	1966	3-light West window
			Two Nave windows
HARBORNE	*SS. Faith and Lawrence*	1959–66	17 lights Apse and Chapel
KINGS HEATH	*Methodist Church*	1963	3-light window in South Wall
	St. Dunstan's	1968	Four windows – slab in resin

NEWBOLD REVEL	*St. Paul's College*	1969	East window – slab in resin
SMALL HEATH	*Holy Family School*	1964	Staircase window
UFTON	*Parish Church*	1964	East window
WARWICK	*St. Nicholas'*	1968	2-light North Aisle appliqué
YARDLEY WOOD	*Our Lady's*	1965	Two 2-light windows in Lady Chapel

WILTSHIRE

TROWBRIDGE	*St. John's Convent*	1967	Frieze round Chapel – slab in resin

WORCESTERSHIRE

AMBLECOTE	*Parish Church*	1965	Third from East South Nave
BROMSGROVE	*Congregational Church*	1968	A. J. Davies Memorial window
GREAT WITLEY	*Parish Church*	1970	Restoration of 18th century Aisle window
MORTON BAGOT	*Parish Church*	1964	East window
WORCESTER	*Royal Infirmary*	1970	Single-light Chapel window
	Shire Hall	1967	Three heraldic panels
WORDSLEY	*Hospital Chapel*	1970	Five lights South Chancel
WRIBBENHALL	*Parish Church*	1961	West of South Aisle

YORKSHIRE

BISHOP THORNTON	*Parish Church*	1969	3-light East window
	St. Joseph's	1959–71	Four Nave windows
DALTON	*Holy Family*	1970	East window and Narthex – slab in resin
EAST HARLSEY	*Parish Church*	1960–70	Three 2-light windows
HUNSLET	*St. Joseph's*	1971	15 hanging panels – slab in resin
NIDD	*Parish Church*	1970	3-light in South Wall
SHEFFIELD	*St. Joseph's*	1950–60	5-light East, 4-light Chapel
	St. Thomas More	1969	3 panels – slab mosaic

WALES

CARDIGANSHIRE

PONTRHYDFENDIGAID	*Community Hall*	1964	Main window

DENBIGHSHIRE

LLANDULAS	*Parish Church*	1964	Single-light

FLINTSHIRE

FLINT	*St. Mary's*	1963–64	5-lights Lady Chapel and Baptistery

GLAMORGANSHIRE

CARDIFF	*Hodge Building*	1966	Screen – slab glass in resin
SWANSEA	*St. David's*	1967–68	Two 2-lights West Wall

MERIONETHSHIRE

DOLGELLAU	*Our Lady's*	1968	Five lights Sanctuary – slab in resin

SCOTLAND

AYRSHIRE

PRESTWICK	*St. Quivox*	1969	East window – slab in concrete

MIDLOTHIAN

EDINBURGH	*National Records Office*	1970	Panel over Entrance – appliqué

RENFREWSHIRE

GREENOCK	*St. Mary's*	1965	One light S.H. Chapel

GUERNSEY

COBO	*St. Matthew's*	1962–68	Four lights in North Wall
ST. PETER PORT	*Parish Church*	1948–60	3-light E. of Lady Chapel
			4-light West
			Four 2-lights

Below left
Parish Church, Haselton, Gloucestershire.

Below right
Parish Church, Lower Gornal, Staffordshire.

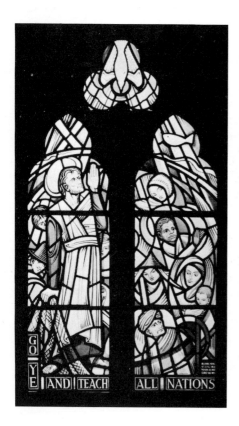

Above left. Holy Family School, Small Heath, Warwickshire.
Above right. International Hotel, Cromwell Road, London.
Below. National Records' Office, Edinburgh, Scotland.

HARRY HARVEY, FMGP
Station House, Barton Hill, York.

DURHAM CO.

DALTON LE DALE	*Parish Church*	1967	Single-light South side
WHEATLEY HILL	*Parish Church*	1961	East window

DERBYSHIRE

WHITTINGTON	*Parish Church*	1969	2-light North side

GLOUCESTERSHIRE

CHELTENHAM	*Christ Church*	1964	Single-light St. George

LANCASHIRE

BLACKBURN	*St. Stephen's, Little Harwood*	1971	Two single-light North side
BURNLEY	*St. Matthew's*	1970	2-light North side
NELSON	*St. Paul's, Little Marsden*	1969	2-light North West corner
WRIGHTINGTON	*Parish Church*	1970	2-light, South West corner

LEICESTERSHIRE

BIRSTALL	*Parish Church*	1968	East window Chapel of All Souls
COALVILLE	*Parish Church*	1963	Single-light South side
COUNTESTHORPE	*Parish Church*	1966	2-light South side
LEICESTER	*Church of the Martyrs*	1962–70	All windows South side
	Kathleen Rutland Home for the Blind	1967	Chapel window
	St. Margaret's	1965	2-light South side
MARKFIELD	*Parish Church*	1963	3-light North side
SHEARSBY	*Parish Church*	1964	2-light South side Chancel
SOMERBY	*Parish Church*	1969	Airborne Forces Memorial

LINCOLNSHIRE

FOTHERBY	*Parish Church*	1966	Single-light South side Chancel
GRANTHAM	*Parish Church*	1963	4-light St. Michael's Chapel
	St. Anne's	1965	East window
MOULTON	*Parish Church*	1966	3-light North side
SPALDING	*Parish Church*	1965	Two 2-lights South side
WESTON	*Parish Church*	1969	Single-light South side Chancel

MONMOUTHSHIRE

NEWPORT	*Christ Church*	1958	East window Lady Chapel

NORTHAMPTONSHIRE

WELLINGBOROUGH	*Wellingborough School*	1962	West window, Chapel
WITTERING	*Parish Church*	1968	R.A.F. Chapel East window
WOODFORD	*Parish Church*	1958	3-light North side

STAFFORDSHIRE

HOPWAS	*Parish Church*	1969	Single-light North West corner

SUFFOLK

GREAT THURLOW	*Parish Church*	1958	East window

WARWICKSHIRE

BIRMINGHAM	*St. Martin's in the Bull Ring*	1957	Chapel of the Holy Rood East window

YORKSHIRE

ADEL	*Parish Church*	1971	Two single-lights Chancel
AISLABY	*(Whitby) Parish Church*	1959	Single-light North side
ALNE	*Parish Church*	1958	East window
AMOTHERBY	*Parish Church*	1970	Single-light South side
APPLETON ROEBUCK	*Parish Church*	1964	2-light North side

ARDSLEY	*Parish Church*	1968	East window
BLACKTOFT	*Parish Church*	1966	2-light, North side
	Parish Church	1971	2-light South side
BOLSTERSTONE	*Parish Church*	1967	2-light North side Chancel
BRIDLINGTON	*Emmanuel Church*	1955	Children's corner window
CAMPSALL	*Parish Church*	1965	East window
CHURCH FENTON	*Parish Church*	1966	Single-light South Transept
CONISBOROUGH	*Parish Church*	1966	2-light North West corner
EASINGTON	*(Hull) Parish Church*	1968	3-light Lady Chapel
EASINGTON	*(Saltburn) Parish Church*	1965	2-light South side
FOSTON ON THE WOLDS	*Parish Church*	1963	East window, North Aisle
HARROGATE	*Woodlands Methodist Church*	1964–68	Two 3-lights North side
HELMSLEY	*Parish Church*	1964	Single-light Porch
HOLLYM	*Parish Church*	1968	3-light South side
HOLME ON SPALDING MOOR	*Parish Church*	1968	Single-light North West corner
HUSTHWAITE	*Parish Church*	1969	2-light South side Chancel
INGLEBY GREENHOW	*Parish Church*	1965	East window
KEXBY	*Parish Church*	1954	East window
KILHAM	*Parish Church*	1967	3-light North side Chancel
KINGSTON-	*St. Mark's*	1964	East window
UPON-HULL	*St. Martin's*	1971	St. George's Chapel window
LEEDS	*Headingley Methodist Church*	1956	2-light North side
	St. Cyprian and St. James	1964	Chancel windows
ROTHERHAM	*Parish Church*	1964	3-light Chapel of Jesus
RUDSTON	*Parish Church*	1956	3-light South side
SHEFFIELD	*Sheffield Cathedral*	1967	6-light St. Katherine's Chapel
	Owlerton Parish Church	1960	Single-light North side
SHELF	*Parish Church*	1964	2-light North side
SKIRPENBECK	*Parish Church*	1967	East window
SPENNITHORNE	*Parish Church*	1966	3-light, North side
STILLINGFLEET	*Parish Church*	1960–69	Two 3-lights North side
STONEGRAVE	*Parish Church*	1961	Heraldic window South Aisle
STRENSALL	*Garrison Church*	1961	East window and Heraldic panel
	Parish Church	1970	2-light North side
SWINEFLEET	*Parish Church*	1961–65–66	Chancel windows and 2-light North side
SWINTON	*(Mexborough) Parish Church*	1966	East window North Aisle
WALKINGTON	*Parish Church*	1970	East window
WESTERDALE	*Parish Church*	1957	2-light South side
WHITBY	*St. Hilda's*	1961	Two 3-lights South side
WILLERBY	*Staxton Parish Church*	1965	Three single-lights North side
WISTOW	*Parish Church*	1959	3-light North Aisle
YORK	*Guildhall*	1960	5-light river front
	St. Hilda's	1959–68–70	East window, two 2-lights in Nave

WALES

RADNORSHIRE

BUILTH WELLS	*Maesmynis Church*	1963	East window and Reredos

BEDFORDSHIRE

SANDY	*Parish Church*	1965	2-light window over Font

BERKSHIRE

ASCOT	*All Saints*	1957	2-light window in Chapel
	Royal Foresters Hotel	1968	Screen in bar Glass appliqué
CHILTON FOLIAT	*Parish Church*	1966	3-light window North Aisle
NEWBURY, WASH COMMON	*St. George*	1965	Large circular West window Circular window, St. Michael's Chapel
WARGRAVE	*Parish Church*	1963	2-light window South Aisle

BUCKINGHAMSHIRE

RAVENSTONE	*All Saints*	1964	3-light East window
STOKE GOLDINGTON	*St. Peter*	1965	2-light window North West corner

CAMBRIDGESHIRE

STUNTNEY, ELY	*Parish Church*	1964	2-light window over Font

DERBYSHIRE

RIPLEY	*All Saints*	1969	3-light East window
SOUTH WINGFIELD	*Parish Church*	1971	Single-light over South Porch

DEVONSHIRE

EXETER	*St. Mary Steps*	1967	3-light East window

DURHAM CO.

WEST HARTLEPOOL	*St. Aidan*	1959	2-light window Lady Chapel
		1961	2-light window North Aisle
		1967	2-light window South Aisle

ESSEX

BECONTREE	*St. Cedd*	1964	East window, abstract glazing
CHELMSFORD	*The Ascension*	1963	East window, abstract glazing
CHINGFORD	*Parish Church*	1965	2-light East window Lady Chapel
ROYDON	*St. Peter*	1970	2-light window, North Side over Altar
WESTCLIFFE ON SEA	*St. Alban*	1971	2-light window North Aisle

GLOUCESTERSHIRE

MITCHELDEAN	*Parish Church*	1970	5-light East window

HAMPSHIRE

OLD BASING	*Parish Church*	1970	3-light window South West corner

HERTFORDSHIRE

CHIPPERFIELD	*Parish Church*	1966	3-light West window
FLAUNDEN	*Parish Church*	1958	3-light East window
LETCHWORTH	*St. Michael*	1969	6 lights in Nave, Glass appliqué
SANDRIDGE	*St. Leonard*	1957	3-light West window

LANCASHIRE

ACCRINGTON	*St. Andrew*	1959	3-light East window, Lady Chapel
BLACKBURN	*Cathedral*	1967	56-light lantern, Glass appliqué
		1968	10-light window South Transept (made from re-cut Victorian glass)

BLACKBURN (continued)	*Cathedral*	1970	4-light East window, St. Martin's Chapel
		1970	Engraved glass screen, St. Martin's Chapel
	St. Jude	1959	4-light East window Lady Chapel
QUERNMORE	*St. Peter*	1959	East Rose window North Chapel
			2-light window North Chapel

LINCOLNSHIRE

GRANTHAM	*Parish Church*	1969	4-light window North Nave
NETTLEHAM	*Parish Church*	1971	5-light East window

LONDON

BLACKHEATH	*Dartmouth House*	1969	Screen in Chapel, Glass appliqué
CITY, CHEAPSIDE	*St. Mary-le-Bow*	1960	Engraved glass screen in Crypt
		1963	Three large East windows
		1964	Two large West windows
CITY, BISHOPSGATE	*Great St. Helen*	1969	5-light West window
			Plain glazing South Nave
CITY, UPPER THAMES STREET	*St. Michael, Paternoster Royal*	1968	Three large East windows
			Abstract glazing North and South Nave
		1969	Dick Whittington window
CITY, HART STREET	*St. Olave*	1970	3-light heraldic window over South entrance
EATON SQUARE	*St. Peter*	1961	All 12 Nave windows
			2-light window North Transept
GLOUCESTER ROAD	*St. Stephen*	1962	East Rose window
GT. ORMOND STREET	*Hospital*	1961	4-lights in lower Chapel
GROSVENOR ROAD SW1	*All Saints*	1958	5-light Apsidal East window
RUSKIN PARK SE	*All Saints*	1961	5-light East window
LONDON FIELDS	*St. Michael*	1961	Twelve lights in West screen
MERTON	*St. James*	1964	Heraldry in Baptistry
		1965	Seven lights at West end
REGENTS PARK	*St. Mark*	1959	2-light window over Organ
		1965	2-light window West end South Aisle
SHADWELL	*St. Paul*	1964	3-light East window
SOHO	*House of Charity Chapel*	1957	All twenty windows
STREATHAM	*Christ Church*	1955	Single-light South Aisle
		1961	East window Lady Chapel
	St. Margaret	1960	2-light window in Chapel
TOOTING BEC	*Bec School*	1955	3-light window over main entrance
WILLESDEN	*St. Andrew*	1964	All ten Nave windows
WEMBLEY	*The Annunciation*	1962	Abstract glazing at East end
WEST HACKNEY	*St. Paul*	1963	5-light West window
NORTH WOOLWICH	*St. John*	1968	Four 2-light windows in Nave

NORFOLK

LITTLE WALSINGHAM	*Parish Church*	1964	10-light East window
	All Souls Chapel	1965	Abstract glazing to octagonal Nave, lantern and Sanctuary

NORTHAMPTONSHIRE

HIGHAM FERRERS	*Parish Church*	1969	Glazed screen and doors West end
			Stain and glass applique
	The Bede House		Heraldry in East window

OXFORDSHIRE

NORTH ASTON	*Parish Church*	1956	Single light in Chancel
OXFORD	*St. Peter's College Chapel*	1964	5-light East window

SURREY

CROYDON	*St. Matthew*	1971	Glass to whole South Wall
BENHILTON (SUTTON)	*All Saints*	1965	3-light West window South Aisle
			3-light window South Aisle and
			tracery in flanking windows
NEW MALDEN	*St. James*	1967	3-light window in porch
PURLEY	*St. Swithun*	1967	Two lights, East end
S. GODSTONE	*St. Stephen*	1960	5-light East window

WARWICKSHIRE

HAMPTON IN ARDEN	*Parish Church*	1967	2-light East window Lady Chapel

NORTHERN IRELAND

BANGOR	*The Abbey*	1961	Engraved glass screen under tower

ABROAD

NEW ZEALAND

INVERCARGILL	*All Saints*	1965	3-light East window
		1970	3-light West window

SOUTH AFRICA

TSOLO	*St. Cuthbert*	1956	3-light apsidal East window
			Six lights in East ambulatory
			Six lights in Nave

TANZANIA

MIFINDI	*Chapel of Tea Company*	1965	Two lights either side Chancel arch

'The Angel of Peace' — Parish Church, Old Basing, Hampshire.

Opposite

Top
St. Michael, Paternoster Royal, Upper Thames Street, London.

Bottom
Dartmouth House, Blackheath, London.

Above left
Parish Church, Chilton Foliat,
Berkshire. St. Hubert Window.

Above right
St. Mary-le-Bow, Cheapside, London.
Detail of East windows.

Left
All Saints, Ravenstone, Buckinghamshire.

Blackburn Cathedral, Lancashire.
South transept window — made entirely from re-cut painted Victorian glass from nave.

D. TAYLOR KELLOCK, DA(Edin) FRSA(Lond) MGP
220 Forest Street, Ballarat, Victoria, Australia

AUSTRALIA

NEW SOUTH WALES

ADAMSTOWN	*St. Stephen's*	1963	Single-light
ALBURY	*Methodist*	1954–64	7-lights Nave
GRAFTON	*Cathedral*	1958	3-light Baptistry
KEMPSEY	*Church of England*	1956–64	3-light West
		1968	Single-light Nave
		1970	2-lights Nave
PARKES	*St. George's*	1956	Great West window

QUEENSLAND

BRISBANE	*St. John's Cathedral*	1960	2-light
		1961	2-light

TASMANIA

BOTHWELL	*Church of England*	1958	Single-light
DEVONPORT	*St. John's C. of E.*	1965	East Rose
			4-lights East
HOBART	*St. David's Cathedral*	1962	2-light Transept
	(Chapel) Royal Hobart Hospital	1967	Single-light
PARATTAH	*St. George's C. of E.*	1955	Single-light
ROWELLA	*St. Stephen's*	1950	Wheel window East
ULVERSTONE	*Church of England*	1970	3-lights

VICTORIA

BALLAN	*St. John's C. of E.*	1956	2-light Nave
BALLARAT	*St. Andrew's*	1954	Single-light Nave
	St. Cuthbert's	1964	Single-light Nave
	St. Paul's C. of E.	1947	2-light Nave
		1953	2-light Nave
		1962	2-light Nave
	St. Peter's C. of E.	1958	2-light Transept
		1962	Single-light Transept
	Skipton Street Methodist	1963	2-light Nave
	Mt. Pleasant Methodist	1965	Single-light Nave
BEAUFORT	*St. Andrew's Presbyterian*	1953	3-light Transept
		1961	Single-light Porch
		1967	2-light Nave
	Methodist Church	1962	Single-light Nave
	St. John's C. of E.	1956	Fifteen windows
BRIGHTON	*St. Andrew's*	1963	6-lights Chapel
CAMBERWELL	*St. John's*	1957–70	Seventeen windows
CARNHAM	*Church of England*	1963	2-light
CRIB POINT	*Naval Depot Chapel*	1953–66	Fifteen windows
LINTON	*St. Paul's C. of E.*	1965	4-lights Nave
MURTOA	*Lutheran Church*	1966	4-light Restoration
PRAHRAN	*Wesley College*	1962	Single-light Nave
		1964	Single-light Nave
RED CLIFFS	*St. Mark's*	1957–60	Seventeen windows
SEBASTOPOL	*St. James' R.C.*	1968	14 Roundels
		1969	2-light
WALLALOO	*Church of England*	1953	Single-light
WAUBRA	*Church of England*	1965	3-light East
		1951	Single-light Nave
		1952	Single-light Nave
		1970	2-light Nave

LAWRENCE LEE
A.R.C.A., HON.D.A. (MANC.), M.G.P.
Stable Cottage, Smart's Hill, Penshurst, Kent

BEDFORDSHIRE

BIGGLESWADE	*St. Andrew's*	1953	3-light window South Aisle
		1954	4-light window Lady Chapel

CHESHIRE

ALDERLEY EDGE	*St. Phillip's*	1965	2-light North Aisle window

CUMBERLAND

CARLISLE	*Wetheral R.C. Chapel*	1962	Two lancets

DERBYSHIRE

MATLOCK	*St. Giles*	1969	East window

DORSET

MILTON ABBAS	*St. James*	1970	East window

ESSEX

SOUTH CHINGFORD	*St. Edmund's*	1953	Transept window
SOUTH WOODFORD	*United Free Church*	1963	Chapel, glass mural and windows
HIGHAMS PARK	*Parish Church*	1963	3-light South Aisle

GLOUCESTERSHIRE

PRESTBURY	*Parish Church*	1967	North and South Aisle windows

HAMPSHIRE

LONGMOOR CAMP	*Garrison Church*	1950	Single-light North Aisle
		1956	West window
		1966	South Aisle single-light
MILTON	*St. James*	1967	Side Chapel 2-light window
KINGSCLERE	*St. Mary's*	1966	Lady Chapel 3-light window

KENT

CATFORD	*St. Andrew's*	1957	Lady Chapel East window
NORTH DULWICH	*St. Faith's*	1957	Lady Chapel window
PENSHURST	*St. John the Baptist*	1970	West window South Aisle
TUNBRIDGE WELLS	*King Charles the Martyr*	1969	North Aisle window

LANCASHIRE

MANCHESTER	*Wythenshawe*	1959	5-light main window
	Unitarian Church		Single-light side window
BLACKPOOL	*St. Paul's*	1964	Two 3-light windows North Aisle
WHITTINGTON	*Parish Church*	1968	South Aisle 2-light window
LYTHAM ST. ANNES	*St. Paul's*	1969	East window

LINCOLNSHIRE

COLSTERWORTH	*Parish Church*	1959	2-light North Aisle
GRIMSBY	*All Saints'*	1965	West window

LONDON

LAMBETH	*St. Andrew's*	1958	Four glass and concrete windows
LOWER THAMES STREET	*St. Magnus the Martyr*	1950	Single-light South Aisle
		1951	Two single-lights South Aisle
		1952	Single-light South Aisle
MARYLEBONE	*Parish Church*	1954	Aisle window
PUTNEY VALE	*Crematorium New Chapel*	1964	West window
SOUTHWARK	*Southwark Cathedral*	1957	Lady Chapel, Rider memorial window

LONDON (continued)

STREATHAM	*St. Peter's*	1954	East window
		1954	Rose window
		1956	Baptistery windows
WATLING STREET	*St. Mary Aldermary*	1952	East window
		1955	East window South Chapel
BATTERSEA	*Sir Walter St. John's School*	1967	Library window
CITY	*Painters/Stainers Hall*	1969	Heraldic window
	Carpenters Hall	1970	Staircase window
SOUTH KENSINGTON	*Science Museum*	1968	Glass Technology mural
PICCADILLY	*Chemical Society*	1968	Staircase windows

MIDDLESEX

HARLESDEN	*Methodist Church*	1957	Main window
HAYES	*St. Edmund's*	1961	Lady Chapel, Chancel and porch glass and concrete windows
RUISLIP	*St. Martin's*	1954	2-light window, Chancel

NORTHAMPTONSHIRE

MEARS ASHBY	*All Saints'*	1970	South Aisle windows

NORTHUMBERLAND

NEWCASTLE UPON TYNE	*Jesmond Parish Church*	1956	East window
		1958	2-light South Aisle

OXFORDSHIRE

OXFORD	*Magdalen College School*	1955	Chapel window heraldic
		1965	Chapel windows glass appliqué

SURREY

BRAMLEY	*Parish Church*	1953	Lancet window North Aisle
CAMBERLEY	*Royal Military Academy, Sandhurst*	1954	George VI memorial West window
		1960–65	South and North Aisle windows
		1965	Lord Alanbrooke Memorial, Chancel
REIGATE	*St. Luke's*	1954	2-light Aisle window
PURLEY	*St. Swithin's*	1954	West Round window
WORCESTER PARK	*St. Mary the Virgin, Cuddington*	1959	West window
CAMBERLEY	*Royal Military Academy, Sandhurst*	1970	Memorial Chapel windows
WORCESTER PARK	*St. Mary the Virgin, Cuddington*	1971	South Aisle two windows
BELMONT	*St. John the Baptist*	1971	East window
ABINGER COMMON	*Parish Church*	1967	East window

SUSSEX

HEENE, WORTHING	*St. Botolph's*	1953	Two lancets North Aisle
HEATHFIELD	*Parish Church*	1962	2-light window North Aisle

Opposite

Top
Church of the Sacred Heart, Leeds, Yorkshire. Sanctuary wall window.

Bottom left
St. John the Baptist, Penshurst, Kent.
Becket Window — commemorating institution of the first priest in 1170 by St. Thomas a Becket.

Bottom right
Parish Church, Abinger Common, Surrey. The Cross as the tree of life.

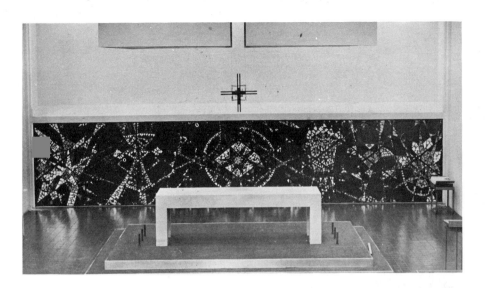

WARWICKSHIRE

COVENTRY	*New Cathedral*	1953	Nave windows (Chief designer on behalf of The Royal College of Art)
BIRMINGHAM	*Saltley Parish Church*	1963	Lady Chapel window
SOLIHULL	*St. Alphege's*	1961	2-light window, Becket Chapel
ATTLEBOROUGH	*Holy Trinity*	1960	East window

YORKSHIRE

*LONG RISTON	*St. Margaret's*	1959	2-light window, North Aisle
*LEEDS	*St. Michael's School Chapel*	1962	Five windows

* In collaboration with Modern Art Glass Company.

LEEDS	*Church of the Sacred Heart*	1965	Glass and resin mural

WALES

CARDIGANSHIRE

ABERYSTWYTH	*St. Michael and All Angels*	1962	2-light South Aisle window

GLAMORGANSHIRE

BETTWS	*Parish Church*	1960	East window

SCOTLAND

LANARKSHIRE

GLASGOW	*University Chapel*		East window

ABROAD

AUSTRALIA

ADELAIDE	*Scots Church*	1962	West window

CANADA

MONTREAL	*St. Andrew and St. Paul General Hospital*	1962–65 .	Ten Clerestory windows Main Hall window

CYPRUS

DHEKALIA	*Garrison Church*	1961–62	Clerestory windows

NEW ZEALAND

AUCKLAND C.I.	*St. Paul's*	1966	East window
	Masonic Village Chapel	1968	East window

SOUTH AFRICA

RONDEBOSCH	*Boys' High School*	1963	Staircase window

TRINIDAD

PORT OF SPAIN	*Christ Church*	1955	East window

C. RUPERT MOORE, ARCA, FMGP
Tykesditch, 36 Oakridge Avenue, Radlett, Hertfordshire
Telephone : Radlett 6576

DORSET
  SHAFTESBURY   *Abbey*   1970   Roundel for Shrine

LINCOLNSHIRE
  BOSTON   *Grammar School*   1969   Series of Figures (made by
                                                              Dennis King of Norwich)

SURREY
  ENGLEFIELD GREEN   *Royal Holloway College*   1972   Chapel window

For many previous designs at home and abroad see under Whitefriars Studios.

St. Mary's Abbey Ruin, Shaftesbury, Dorset. Roundel to mark the spot where remains of Edward, King and Martyr were rediscovered after being hidden by Abbess during the Reformation.

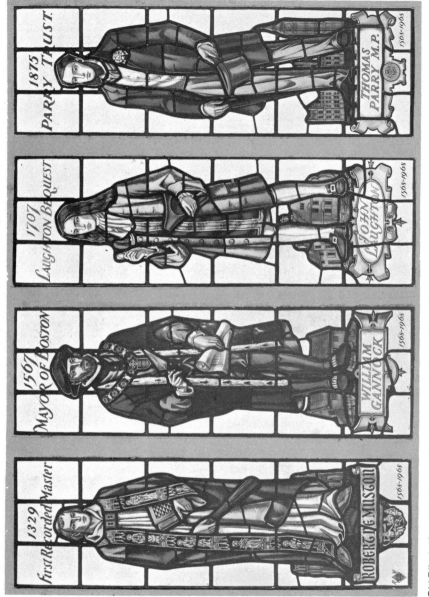

Old Elizabethan Hall, Boston Grammar School, Lincolnshire. Four School Dignitaries.

74

EDITH NORRIS, FRRGC, AMGP
656 Tonge Moor Road, Bolton, Lancashire

LANCASHIRE

BOLTON			
	Congregational Church,	1970	3-light South Aisle
	St. George's Road		
	St. Margaret's of	1968	3-light North Aisle
	Scotland, Lonsdale Road		

Left

Congregational Church, St. Georges Road, Bolton, Lancashire.
One of a set of four windows to the Leverhulme family — this one to grandsons
J.L. and F.L. Tillotson and their wives.

Right

St. Margaret's of Scotland, Lonsdale Road, Bolton, Lancashire.
In memory of Stephen Kyle 1875-1966.

CANADA

NEW BRUNSWICK

AROOSTIC JUNCTION	*United Baptist Church*	1966	One single-light Nave window
BERWICK	*United Church of Canada*	1970	Three 2-light Nave windows
FLORENCEVILLE	*United Church of Canada*	1969	One single-light Nave window
FREDERICTON	*Gibson Memorial United Church*	1970	One single-light Nave window
MACTAQUAC	*United Baptist Church*	1966	One 2-light window above Main Door
MILLTON	*St. George Anglican Church*	1967	One 3-light Nave window
MACES BAY	*Anglican*	1970	One single-light Nave window
	United Baptist	1970	One single-light Nave window
NASHWAAKSIS	*United Church of Canada*	1966–67	One 3-light Chapel window One 2-light Chapel window
NEW MARYLAND	*United Church of Canada*	1966	Five single-light Nave windows
NORTON	*United Church of Canada*	1969	Two single-light Nave windows
SAINT JOHN	*First Baptist Church*	1966	One 3-light window above Baptistery
	Germain Street Baptist Church	1968	24-light Lantern Tower window
	Park Avenue United Church	1968	One single-light Nave window
	Portland United Church	1968	One single-light Chapel window
	St. Mark's United Church	1965–70	Five 3-light Nave windows and three Nave windows still in progress Ten single-light Narthex windows One 2-light Narthex window
	St. Vincent Convent Chapel	1968	14 lights in Balcony window
	Waterloo Street Baptist Church	1967	Two single-light Nave windows
SOUTH BAY	*United Church of Canada*	1968	One single-light Nave window
TAY SETTLEMENT	*Stanley United Church*	1968	One single-light Nave window

NEWFOUNDLAND

BRIGUS	*United Church of Canada*	1969	One single-light Nave window

NOVA SCOTIA

BROOKFIELD	*United Church of Canada*	1967–70	Four panels Nave
FLORENCE	*United Church of Canada*	1969	One single-light Nave window
NEW WATERFORD	*United Church of Canada*	1966–67	Two single-light Nave windows
	Anglican	1967	One single-light Nave window
PORT MEDWAY	*United Baptist Church*	1967	One single-light Nave window
SYDNEY MINES	*Carmen United Church*	1965	One single-light Nave window

PRINCE EDWARD ISLAND

BEDEQUE	*United Church of Canada*	1970	One 3-light Nave window
CHARLOTTETOWN	*Royal Park United Church*	1967	One 2-light Nave window
MONTAQUE	*St. Andrew's Presbyterian*	1967	One single-light Nave window
MURRAY HARBOUR	*St. John's United Church*	1967	One 2-light Nave window

NEW BRUNSWICK

SLAB GLASS IN EPOXY RESIN

SAINT JOHN	*Apartment building*	1968	Two single-light windows
SUSSEX	*St. Paul's United Church*	1969	One 10-light Transept window
WESTFIELD	*Private home*	1968	One single-light window

GLASS APPLIQUE

SAINT JOHN	*Portland United Church*	1970	One 3-light Tower window
	Stella Maris R.C. Church	1970	One 3-light Balcony window
SUSSEX	*St. Paul's United Church*	1969	Two single-light Nave windows and still in progress

RESTORATION

SAINT JOHN	*Centenary Queen Square United Church*	1965	All existing windows work still in progress
	Germain Street Baptist	1968	All existing windows
	Portland United Church	1970	All existing windows
	St. Andrew and St. David United Church	1965	Seven Chapel windows
	St. John Mission Church	1969	All existing windows
SUSSEX	*Sussex Baptist Church*	1967	All existing windows

ENGLAND

DEVONSHIRE

BARNSTAPLE	*North Devon Crematorium*	1970	One artificially lit panel
GOODLIGH	*Anglican Church*	1960	One single-light Nave window

DEVONSHIRE
EXETER | *House of Professor the Rev. W. M. Merchant* | 1960 | St. Christopher panel

MONMOUTHSHIRE
MYNYDDISLWYN | *St. Tudwal's* | 1970 | Single window, centre of South Wall

NEWPORT | *Trinity Methodist Church* 1969 | Two main East windows

STAFFORDSHIRE
WEST BROMWICH | *St. James's* | 1963 | Single window, South Wall

SUSSEX
BRIGHTON | *Brighton and Hove New Synagogue* | 1967 1968 1969 | Two 11 ft doors to the Ark 5-light centre window, East Wall Two 5-light windows, right and left, East Wall

WALES

CARDIFF
BUTE TERRACE | *Wales Gas Board H.Q.* | 1963 | Glass and resin panel for the Computer Area

CARMARTHENSHIRE
LLANDOVERY | *Llanfair-ar-y-Bryn* | 1965 | 2-light window, South Chancel

GLAMORGANSHIRE
BRITON FERRY | *Our Lady of the Assumption* | 1966 | Sixteen panels in the Narthex Screen

CAERAU | *St. Cynfelin's* | 1961 | Single window, North Chancel

COLWINSTON | *St. Michael's* | 1963 | 3-light window, South Wall

GORSEINON | *Church of the Blessed Sacrament* | 1967 1968 | Eight cross windows for the Chapel Eight cross windows for the Baptistery

NANTYFFYLLON | *St. Peter's* | 1962 1967 | Single window, North Wall Two single windows, North and South Walls

PENARTH | *Trevethin, Clinton Road* 1964 | Two commemorative panels for Dr. Guy

All Saints' | 1966 | 2-light window, North Wall

PONTYCLUN | *St. Paul's* | 1965 | 2-light window, North Wall

ABROAD

U.S.A.
BIRMINGHAM, ALABAMA | *16th Street Baptist Church* | 1965 | Main West window Gift to the bombed Negro church from the people of Wales

'The Alabama Window' — Negro Church in Birmingham, Alabama, U.S.A.

HUGH POWELL

Main Studio Farringdon Hurst, Alton, Hants.   *Telephone:* Tisted 210
London Studio *Telephone:* 01 736 3113
Designer and maker of stained glass windows for traditional and new buildings

HAMPSHIRE

POOLE	*General Hospital Chapel*	A window of unusual shape for a new setting carried out in hand-made glass and epoxy resin
IFORD, NEAR CHRISTCHURCH	*St. Saviour's Church*	A large East window containing Nativity, Crucifixion and Resurrection. Traditional painted and leaded glass

KENT

ST. MARY CRAY	*St. Philomenas' Convent School*	A large 10-light window in a new Chapel. Carried out in hand-made glass and epoxy resin

OXFORDSHIRE

OXFORD	*County Hall*	Coat of arms in Chairmans office, traditional painted and leaded glass

SURREY

BURGH HEATH NEAR EPSOM	*St. Mark's Church*	A 3-light Transom window for a new church carried out in hand-made glass and epoxy resin. Also an abstract area of leaded glass at East end

SUSSEX

BURGESS HILL	*St. Edward's Church*	A slender decorative window for a new church. Carried out in hand-made glass and epoxy resin. Also a range of simple decorative leaded windows in West Wall
WOODINGDEAN	*Church of the Holy Cross*	A tall single-light window for a modern church carried out in hand-made glass and epoxy resin

WILTSHIRE

WARMINSTER	*St. Giles' Garrison Church, School of Infantry*	Two large areas of rich abstract colour in a modern setting. Leaded hand-made glass

YORKSHIRE

APPLETON LE STREET		Small 3-light window containing heraldry and St. Hubert. Traditional painted and leaded glass

A more detailed list of work for specific areas can be supplied.

Opposite

Top
Appleton-le-Street, Nr. Malton, Yorkshire.

Bottom left
'Parable' Window, St. Philomena's Convent, St. Mary Cray, Orpington, Kent.

Bottom right
St. John's Church, Boscombe, Hampshire.

80

PAUL QUAIL, AMGP
28 Mount Ararat Road, Richmond, Surrey

Paul Quail, Designer Craftsman in Stained Glass, is a member of the Society of Designer-Craftsmen, an Associate Member of the Society of Master Glass Painters, and on the approved list of artists of the National Council of Industrial Design.

GLOUCESTERSHIRE
CIRENCESTER · *Royal Agricultural College Chapel* · 1962 · East window

KENT
TUNBRIDGE WELLS · *Chapel of Sacred Heart Convent* · 1967 · Two abstract concrete and glass windows, and two abstract glass appliqué windows

LANCASHIRE
BRYN, NEAR WIGAN · *St. Peter's Church* · 1966 · Large abstract window

LONDON
CHISWICK · *St. Joseph's Church, Bolton Road* · 1960 · Two single-light windows

HARRINGAY · *St. Augustine's Church* · 1965 · Baptistery window (glass appliqué)

LENNOX GARDENS · *St. Simon Zelotes Church* · Two single-light windows

STAFFORDSHIRE
STOKE-ON-TRENT · *St. Werbergh's Church* · 1969 · 2-light window

SURREY
WOKINGHAM · *Shoe shop* · 1968 · Large abstract panels in slab glass set in epoxy resin.

SUSSEX
ARDINGLY · *Ardingly College* · 1971 · 3-light abstract window

YORKSHIRE
SKELTON · *Parish Church* · 1970 · 3-light window

ABROAD

SOUTH AFRICA
PORT ELISABETH · *St. Nicholas' Church* · 1968 · Single-light window

Chapel, Convent of Sacred Heart, Tunbridge Wells, Kent.

PATRICK REYNTIENS
Burleighfield House, Loudwater, Buckinghamshire

Born London 1925.
Educated Ampleforth College 1940–43.
Army Career 1943–47.
Marylebone School of Art 1947–50.
Edinburgh College of Art 1950–52.
Learnt Stained Glass under J. E. Nuttgens 1952–54.
As well as designing and making his own stained glass he has made all glass to the designs of John Piper. He has also made glass to designs from Ceri Richards, Brian Young and Philip Sutton.
In most of the work listed by all designers he has been helped by Derek White who has supervised all leaded glass since 1958, and by David Kirby who has been responsible for technical supervision of Liverpool Cathedral and many other works. He has been generally helped by Charles Broome.
Patrick Reyntiens has work in private collections in England and America. He has contributed twice to Arts Council Exhibitions of stained glass. Has had one-man shows of glass in Edinburgh, London, Reading. Has contributed to other mixed exhibitions. Is the author of a definitive book on the technique of stained glass. He is on the Advisory panel of Decoration to Westminster Cathedral and the Brompton Oratory, is a member of the Craft Advisory Commission and a member of the Court of the Royal College of Art.

BEDFORDSHIRE

TOTTERNHOE	*St. Giles'*	1970–71	3-light East window Designer: John Piper

BERKSHIRE

ETON	*College Chapel*	1958–61	Eight Nave windows Designer: John Piper Technical supervisor: Derek White Architect in charge: Sir William Holford
WINDSOR CASTLE	*St. George's Chapel* *George VI Memorial Chapel*	1969	Designer: John Piper Technical Supervisor: Derek White Architects: George Pace & Paul Paget

BUCKINGHAMSHIRE

BLEDLOW RIDGE	*St. Paul's*	1968	West window Designer: John Piper
FLACKWELL HEATH	*Christ Church*	1962	Rose window Designer: Patrick Reyntiens Architect: Sebastian Comper

CAMBRIDGESHIRE

BABRAHAM	*St. Peter's*	1966	East window Designer: John Piper Architect in charge: Marshall Sisson
CAMBRIDGE	*Churchill College*	1970	Eight windows of Chapel Designer: John Piper Technical Supervisor: Derek White Architects: Richard Sheppard, Robson & Partners

DERBYSHIRE

DERBY	*Cathedral*	1964–65	Two side-aisle West windows, All Souls & All Saints Designer: Ceri Richards, CBE Technical Supervisor: Derek White Architect in charge: Sebastian Comper
EDNASTON	*St. Mary's Nursing Home*	1965	Both Nave ranges of windows Designer: Patrick Reyntiens Architect: William Blair & Partners

DEVONSHIRE

PLYMOUTH	*St. Andrew's*	1962	West window, the Astor Memorial window
		1963	East window
		1965–66	Lady Chapel window St. Catherine's Chapel window
		1968	North and South Transept windows Designer: John Piper Technical Supervisor: Derek White Architect in charge: Frederick Etchells

DORSET

BRANKSOME PARK, POOLE	*Oratory Preparatory School*	1964	3-light window in Chapel Designer: Patrick Reyntiens

GLOUCESTERSHIRE

BRISTOL	*Clifton School Chapel*	1964	2-light window Designer: Patrick Reyntiens

HAMPSHIRE

HOUNDS	*St. Mary's*	1962	3-light window Designer: Patrick Reyntiens Architect: Robert Bostock & Partners
ODIHAM	*All Saints*	1968 1969	West window Lady Chapel window Designer: Patrick Reyntiens
WINCHESTER	*Wessex Hotel*	1964	Twelve decorative panels Designer: John Piper Architects: Fielden & Mawson
HINTON AMPNER	*Parish Church*	1970	Two East windows Designer: Patrick Reyntiens

KENT

MARDEN		1963	3-light East window and two smaller side windows Designer: Patrick Reyntiens

LANCASHIRE

LEYLAND	*St. Mary's Priory*	1964–65	Total glazing of Church in Dalle-de-Verre Designer: Patrick Reyntiens Technical Supervisor: David Kirby Architect: Weightman & Bullen with George Faczinski

LIVERPOOL	*Metropolitan Cathedral of Christ the King*	1965–67	Lantern, Nave windows and some site Chapel windows Dalle-de-Verre Designers: John Piper and Patrick Reyntiens Technical Supervisor: David Kirby Architect: Frederick Gibberd & Partners
	Metropolitan Cathedral Lady Chapel	1967	Two side windows Designer: Ceri Richards, CBE Technical Supervisor: Derek White Architect in charge: John Forrest
	St. Christopher's Grange	1970	Total glazing of the Chapel in Dalle-de-Verre Designer: Patrick Reyntiens
		1971	Five contemplative panels Dalle-de-Verre Designer: Patrick Reyntiens Technique devised by Charles Broome
LONDON			
WESTMINSTER	*St. Margaret's*	1967–68	Eight Nave windows Designer: John Piper
BERNERS STREET	*Sanderson's Store*	1959–60	Interior mural on staircase Designer: John Piper Technical Supervisor: Derek White Architect: Slater & Uren
TWICKENHAM	*St. Margaret's*	1968–69	Baptistery and East window Designer: Patrick Reyntiens Architect: Williams & Winkley
	Baker's Company Livery Hall	1968–69	Three decorative panels Designer: John Piper Architect: Trehearne, Norman Preston & Partners
FULHAM	*Private Chapel, Oratory School*	1970	Designer: Patrick Reyntiens Architect: David Stokes and Partners
HOLLAND PARK	*Private Chapel at No. 58*	1970	Designer: Patrick Reyntiens Architect: Williams & Winkley
SOUTHALL	*St. Anselm's*	1971	East window Designer: Patrick Reyntiens Architect: Burles Newton & Partners
MONMOUTHSHIRE			
NEWPORT	*St. Woolo's Cathedral*	1964	East End Rose window Designer: John Piper Architects: Caroe & Partners
NORFOLK			
SCOLE	*All Saints' Parish Church*	1965	East window Designer: Patrick Reyntiens Architect: Fielden & Mawson
NORTHAMPTONSHIRE			
OUNDLE	*School Chapel*	1954–56	Three East windows Designer: John Piper
PETERBOROUGH	*Chapel of the Bishop's Palace*	1958	Three small windows Designer: Patrick Reyntiens

NORTHAMPTONSHIRE (continued)

WELLINGBOROUGH	*All Hallows'*	1962	East window, North Aisle
		1964	Rose window, West End
		1969	South Aisle, Nave window
			Designer: John Piper

NOTTINGHAMSHIRE

HUCKNALL	*Catholic Church*	1961–62	Nineteen windows in Lady Chapel
			Designer: Patrick Reyntiens
WOODTHORPE	*Church of the Good Shepherd*	1964–65	Total Church glazed in Dalle-de-Verre
			Designer: Patrick Reyntiens
			Technical Supervisor: David Kirby
			Architect: Gerard Goalen
MISTERTON	*Parish Church*	1966	Left-hand East window
			Designer: John Piper

OXFORDSHIRE

OXFORD	*Nuffield College Chapel*	1965–66	Five windows
			Designer: John Piper
			Architect: Harrison, Barnes & Hubbard
PISHILL		1969	Small lancet window
			Designer: John Piper

STAFFORDSHIRE

WOLVERHAMPTON	*St. Andrew's*	1968	7-light window at West End
			Designer: John Piper
			Technical Supervisor: Derek White
			Architect: Twentyman & Partners

SUSSEX

ST. LEONARDS-ON-SEA	*Parish Church*	1957	Eleven windows
			Designer: Patrick Reyntiens
			Architect: Adrian Gilbert Scott

WARWICKSHIRE

COVENTRY	*Coventry Cathedral*	1959–62	Great Baptistery window
			Designer: John Piper
			Technical Supervisor: Derek White
			Architect: Sir Basil Spence & Partners

YORKSHIRE

SHEFFIELD	*St. Mark's*	1963–64	West window
			Designer: John Piper
			Architect: George Pace
AMPLEFORTH	*Lady Chapel, Ampleforth Abbey*	1963	2-light window
			Designer: Patrick Reyntiens
			Architect: Sir Giles Gilbert Scott
	Malsis School	1967	Two ranges of windows in Chapel Chancel
			Designer: John Piper

WALES

SWANSEA	*St. Mary's Church*	1965–66	2-light Lady Chapel windows Designer: John Piper
LLANDAFF	*Cathedral*	1961–62	3-light East window high above Altar Designer: John Piper Architect in charge: George Pace

EIRE

WATERFORD	*St. Joseph's Church*	1966–68	Total glazing in Dalle-de-Verre Designer: Patrick Reyntiens Technical Supervisor: David Kirby Architect: O'Neill, Flanagan
	Sacred Heart Church	1967–69	Total glazing in Dalle-de-Verre Designer: Patrick Reyntiens Technical Supervisor: David Kirby and Derek White Architect: O'Neill, Flanagan
	Blessed Sacrament Chapel	1968–69	North and South windows Designer: Patrick Reyntiens Architect: O'Neill Flanagan

ABROAD

NEW ZEALAND

CHRISTCHURCH	*Cathedral*	1968	Small 2-light window Designer: John Piper

SOUTH AFRICA

JOHANNESBURG	*Unicorn Building*	1968	Four large decorative panel windows Designer: Patrick Reyntiens Technical Supervisor: Derek White Architect: John Fassler & Partners
	St. George's, Parktown	1963–64	4-light East window Designer: Brian Young Technical Supervisor: Derek White Architect: Fleming, Cooke and Walker

U.S.A.

WASHINGTON	*Episcopalian Cathedral*	1968–69	3-light General White memorial window Designer: Patrick Reyntiens Technical Supervisor: Derek White Architect: George Bodley and Philip Frohman

ROSEMARY ELLEN RUTHERFORD, AMGP
The Priory, Walsham-le-Willows, Bury St. Edmunds, Suffolk

ESSEX

BRADFIELD	*St. Lawrence's Church*	1960	Two windows, North Wall The Light of the World Christ blessing children
BROOMFIELD	*St. Mary's Church*	1951	South Wall The Raising of Lazarus
		1952	East window The Resurrection
		1956	South Wall Christ washing the disciples feet
		1966	South Wall Christ and the Samaritan woman at the Well
CLACTON ON SEA	*St. Paul's Church*	1965	Slab glass and concrete The conversion of St. Paul
HALSTEAD	*Roman Catholic Church*	1955	East window The Good Shepherd
NEVENDON	*St. Peter's Church*	1950	East window The Transfiguration
TENDRING	*St. Edmund's Church*	1967	Chancel window The Annunciation

LANCASHIRE

ASPULL NEAR WIGAN	*St. Elizabeth's Church*	1968	South Wall The Transfiguration

LEICESTERSHIRE

SAXELBY	*St. Peter's Church*	1959	East window, South Aisle Life of St. Peter
GRIMSTON	*St. John the Baptist's Church*	1966	East window Three Saints

LONDON

CITY ROAD	*Moorfields Eye Hospital Chapel*	1971	Two slab and concrete windows Celtic Cross and Angel

NORFOLK

GAYWOOD NEAR KING'S LYNN	*St. Faith's Church*	1966	East window, South Transept Harvest parable

OXFORDSHIRE

BERINSFIELD	*St. Mary and St. Berin*	1961	Four slab and concrete windows The Sacraments

RUTLAND

PRESTON	*St. Peter and St. Paul*	1962	South Chancel window Nativity

SURREY

	Charterhouse Memorial Chapel	1964	North Porch Three slab and concrete symbolic panels
GUILDFORD	*Cathedral*	1955	North Wall of Chancel The Charterhouse window
MERTON PARK	*Methodist Church*	1958	Three Bible windows

SUSSEX

WORTHING	*Offington Park Methodist Church*	1959	Three Grisaille windows, The Wall, The Tree of Life, The River of God

WARWICKSHIRE
BARTLEY GREEN | *St. Michael's Church* | 1965 | Slab and concrete symbolic Lancet windows

WORCESTERSHIRE
SEDGLEY | *All Saints' Church* | 1971–72 | St. Hubert and the Madonna and Child

YORKSHIRE
WEST HESLERTON | *All Saints' Church* | 1966 | West Wall Flower window

BROMPTON BY SAWDON | *All Saints' Church* | 1970 | North Wall Bird window

ABROAD

NEW ZEALAND
NORTH ISLAND
HAVELOCK NORTH | *Woodford House School* | 1961 | South Wall, Flower Window
HEREWORTH | *School Chapel* | 1964 | Slab and concrete circular East window Rock and Eagle

SOUTH ISLAND | *Hanmer Church* | 1966 | Apse windows St. Andrew and St. Luke

Left
St. Faith's Church,
Gaywood,
Nr. Kings Lynn,
Norfolk.

Right
St. Edmund's
Church, Tendring,
Essex.

SHRIGLEY & HUNT LIMITED
John O'Gaunts Studio, 43 West Road, Lancaster

CHESHIRE
HANMER	*Parish Church*	In hand	2-light window

LANCASHIRE
BLACKBURN	*St. Phillip's*	1970	Single-light window
BRADSHAW	*St. Maxentius*	1970	3-light window
CHIPPING	*Parish Church*	1970	3-light window
CHORLEY	*St. Peter's*	1971	2-light window
HIGHER WALTON		In hand	4-light window
HOGHTON	*Parish Church*	1971	3-light window
LEIGH	*Bedford Parish Church*	1970	3-light window
MORECAMBE	*St. Barnabas'*	1971	3-light window
SILVERDALE	*St. John's*	1971	Single-light window

LONDON
WOOD GREEN	*St. Paul's*	1970	Restoration 19 windows

STAFFORDSHIRE
BASFORD	*St. Mark's*	1970	2-light window

WESTMORLAND
KENDAL	*St. Thomas'*	1970	East window

EIRE

DONEGAL
PETTIGO	*Templecarne*	1970	East window double tier

NORTHERN IRELAND

ANTRIM
BELFAST	*Cregah Parish Church*	In hand	West window

ARMAGH
PORTADOWN	*St. Mark's*	1971	3-light window

FERMANAGH
ENNISKILLEN	*Garvary Church*	In hand	West window

WALES

FLINTSHIRE
SHOTTON	*Parish Church*	In hand	Single-light window

Opposite

Top left
Parish Church, Hoghton, Lancashire. Design by H. W. Harvey.

Top right
Lady Chapel, St. Barnabas' Church, Morecambe, Lancashire.
Design by H. W. Harvey.

Bottom left
Church of St. Thomas More, Sheffield, Yorkshire. Design by Joseph Fisher.

Bottom right
Parish Church, Chipping, Lancashire. Design by Joseph Fisher.

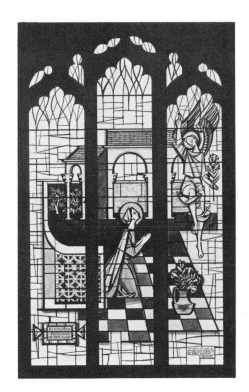

FRANCIS W. SKEAT, FBSMGP, FRSA
5 Cross Lane, Harpenden, Hertfordshire
Telephone : Harpenden 4747

CAMBRIDGESHIRE
LITTLEPORT	*Parish Church*	1967	Fitch Memorial
SWAVESEY	*Parish Church*	1967	Lady Chapel East window

DERBYSHIRE
SOMERCOTES	*Parish Church*	1961	Lady Chapel East window
WINSHILL	*Parish Church*	1960	St. Cecilia

ESSEX
EASTWOOD	*St. Lawrence*	1964	St. Lawrence
FRINTON ON SEA	*St. Mary Mag.*	1969	Conversion of St. Paul
HADLEIGH	*St. Barnabas'*	1964	Two 3-light windows
WESTCLIFF	*St. Michael*	1969	Epiphany window

HAMPSHIRE
ROWNER	*St. Mary's*	1969	St. John the Baptist

LANCASHIRE
FARNWORTH	*St. James', New Bury*	1966	Nativity
OLDHAM	*St. Barnabas'*	1970	East window
ROCHDALE	*St. Anne's, Belfield*	1965	West window
WHITE MOSS	*St. Mark's, Blackley*	1969	Chancel windows

LEICESTERSHIRE
MEASHAM	*Parish Church*	1962	North and South East windows

LINCOLNSHIRE
LINCOLN	*The Cathedral*	1969	Over Russell Chantry

LONDON
HOLBORN	*St. Sepulchre's*	1968	Capt. John Smith Memorial

NOTTINGHAMSHIRE
EDINGLEY	*Parish Church*	1964	East window

STAFFORDSHIRE
PENSNETT	*St. Mark's*	1966	Chapel windows

SUSSEX
LURGASHALL	*Parish Church*	1967	St. Lawrence window

WORCESTERSHIRE
HAGLEY. W.	*St. Saviour's*	1962	East and West windows
UPTON SNODSBURY	*Parish Church*	1968	East window and single window

YORKSHIRE
HUBBERHOLME	*Parish Church*	1971	South window, Nave

Lincoln Cathedral.
The Angel Choir — over
the Russell Chantry

Longparish Church,
Nr. Andover, Hampshire.
North wall of nave.

BEDFORDSHIRE

HARROLD	*St. Peter's*	1952	3-light East window

CHESHIRE

ELLESMERE PORT	*Christ Church*	1957	2-light East window in Chapel

CORNWALL

PAR	*The Good Shepherd*	1954	5-light East window

DERBYSHIRE

CHURCH GRESLEY	*SS. George and Mary*	1952	Four roundels in Nave windows

DEVONSHIRE

CROWNHILL	*The Ascension*	1968	Engraved glass doors

ESSEX

BLACK NOTLEY	*SS. Peter and Paul*	1952	3-light East window
BROXTED	*St. Mary's*	1967	3-light East window in St. John's Chapel
LEIGH-ON-SEA	*St. Clement's*	1971	3-light window, North Aisle
		1971	2-light window opposite porch
	St. Margaret's	1950	3-light East window
NORTH WEALD	*St. Andrew's*	1967	3-light East window
WALTHAM ABBEY	*The Abbey*	1966	East window of North Aisle 900th Anniversary of the Founding Memorial

GLOUCESTERSHIRE

COLEFORD	*St. John's*	1958	2-light East window
CONEY HILL	*St. Oswald*	1954	3-light East window in Chapel

HAMPSHIRE

ALRESFORD	*St. John Baptist*	1956	2-light window in South Aisle

HERTFORDSHIRE

COTTERED	*St. John Baptist*	1954	Single-light in North Chapel
MONKEN HADLEY	*St. Mary's*	1951	3-light East window

KENT

CROCKHAM HILL	*Holy Trinity*	1967	2-light window, North Wall of Chancel
PLUCKLEY	*St. Nicholas'*	1954	3-light East window
SHOREHAM	*SS. Peter and Paul*	1953	3-light East window
SUTTON VALANCE	*School*	1951	Three large heraldic windows in Hall
UPPER HARDRES	*SS. Peter and Paul*	1971	2-light window in Lady Chapel

LINCOLNSHIRE

DEEPING ST. JAMES	*St. James'*	1966	East window
HOLBEACH	*All Saints'*	1951	3-light window, North Aisle
MOULTON	*All Saints'*	1953	3-light Moulton School window in North Aisle

LONDON

BLACKHEATH	*Roan School*	1949	The School Arms, in Library
CITY	*National Bank of Scotland, Lombard Street*	1955	Heraldic window in Banking Hall
SMITHFIELD	*St. Bartholomew's*	1969	Heraldic Panel in Knights Bachelor Shrine window

HIGHGATE	*School Chapel*	1953	2-light window on South side
HOXTON	*St. John Baptist*	1958	East window
		1959	East window of Chapel
			Children's window
			Font window
LAMBETH	*St. Mary's*	1953–58	5-light East window,
			The Pedlar window
			Baptistery window
			West windows (Lambeth
			Conference Memorial)
ROTHERHITHE	*St. Bartholomew's*	1953	Single-light window in Lady
			Chapel
UPPER NORWOOD	*St. Margaret's*	1968	Circular abstract window and
			illuminated glass cross
VICTORIA DOCKS	*The Ascension*	1969	2-light window in North Aisle
WESTMINSTER	*United Westminster Schools*	1949	Five Heraldic panels in The Governors' Room

MIDDLESEX
ALPERTON	*St. James'*	1951	2-light window in North Chapel
HARLINGTON	*SS. Peter and Paul*	1954	Two single-light and two 3-light windows in North Aisle
HAYES	*St. Mary's*	1954	3-light East window in North Chapel
PERIVALE	*Old Church of St. Mary*	1968	3-light East window

MONMOUTHSHIRE
MONMOUTH	*Monmouth School*	1950	2-light window in War Memorial Shrine
	St. Peter's, Dixton	1953	3-light East window

NOTTINGHAMSHIRE
PLEASLEY	*St. Michael's*	1967	2-light West window

SHROPSHIRE
WROCKWARDINE WOOD	*Holy Trinity*	1956	Apse window and two single-lights at West End

SUFFOLK
IPSWICH	*St. Luke's*	1969	3-light East window

SURREY
CROYDON	*Mayday Hospital*	1961	Single-light window in Chapel
KINGSWOOD	*St. Andrew's*	1954–57	Four 2-light Nave windows

SUSSEX
WILMINGTON	*SS. Mary and Peter*	1960	Single-light in Lady Chapel

WARWICKSHIRE
RUGBY	*St. Peter's*	1955	5-light East window

YORKSHIRE
ALTOFTS	*Parish Church*	1969	2-light West window
CUDWORTH	*St. John's*	1969	3-light window in North Aisle
DANBY	*Fryup Chapel*	1957	3-light East window
HARROGATE	*St. Wilfrid's*	in progress	Large single-light in Chapel of the Holy Spirit
HARTHILL	*All Hallows*	1952	3-light East window in Chapel
HULL	*The Transfiguration*	1954	3-light East window
	St. Aidan	1957–60	Six single-light windows in Nave
KIRBYMOORSIDE	*St. Mary's*	1953	2-light window in North Aisle
SCALBY	*St. Laurence*	1960	3-light East window
WAKEFIELD	*Pinderfields Hospital*	1970	3-light East window in Chapel
			Two single-light windows
YORK	*St. Thomas'*	1956	3-light East window

RENFREWSHIRE
PAISLEY   *The Abbey*   1955   4-light East window in St.
                                                           Mirin's Aisle

WALES

CAERNARVONSHIRE
CAERNARVON   *Cwmfrydd*   1956   2-light East window

FLINTSHIRE
ST. ASAPH   *Corwen*   1970   3-light window in South Aisle

ABROAD

FRANCE
MARSEILLES   *Private Chapel of the*   1948   Two windows
                         Argenti Family

HAWAII
PAAUILO   *St. Columba*   1956   Nave window

SOUTH AFRICA
KRUGERSDORP   *St. Peter's*   1969   Seven Nave lights

Below left
St. Margaret's Church, Upper Norwood, London.

Below
School Hall, Sutton Valence, Kent.

Pinderfields Hospital Chapel, Wakefield, Yorkshire.

CAROLINE M. SWASH (MRS.)

113 Albert Palace Mansions
Lurline Gardens
London SW11

Triangle
Box
near Stroud
Gloucestershire

Born 1941. Father (Edward Payne) and grandfather (the late Henry Payne) both stained glass artists.
Educated : Gloucestershire College of Art and Institute of Education, London University.

HERTFORDSHIRE

POTTERS BAR | *Mount Grace Comprehensive School* | 1966 | Interior Screen (not illustrated)

ABROAD

U.S.A.
OHIO

CLEVELAND	*Collection of Professor and Mrs. Victor Radcliffe*	1967	Abstract indoor panel
	St. Paul's Church	1967	'Resurrection' 5-light West window
		1968	'Ichthys' Baptistery panel 'Dove' and 'Fish' two Nave windows
		1969	'Abstract' 4-light Clerestory window
		1970	'The Stoning of Stephen' 4-light Clerestory window
		in progress	'Vision on the Road to Damascus' 4-light Clerestory window

Cleveland Heights, Ohio, U.S.A.
(Private ownership)

98

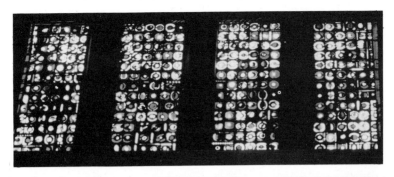

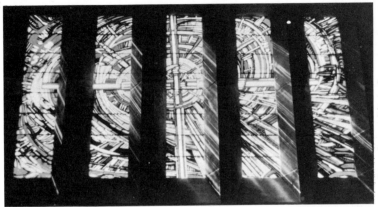

St. Paul's Church, Cleveland, Ohio, U.S.A.
Clerestory window *(top)*, 'Resurrection' *(centre)*, 'Ichthys' *(bottom)*.

99

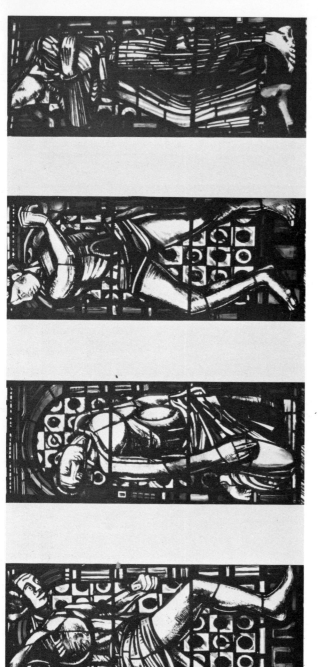

St. Paul's Church, Cleveland, Ohio, U.S.A. 'The Stoning of Stephen'.

BRIAN D. L. THOMAS, OBE, FMGP
The Studio, 3 Hill Road, London NW8
Telephone: 01 286 0804
Rome Scholar in Mural Painting; Past Master Art Workers Guild; former Principal, Byam Shaw School

Note: All stained glass work in collaboration with the Whitefriars Studios, Wealdstone, Kent.

BERKSHIRE

WINDSOR CASTLE	*St. George's Chapel*	Eight painted glass panels inset in altar rails, 'Symbols of the Kingdom of Heaven'
TIDMARSH	*Tidmarsh Church*	Biographical memorial to Sir Harold Graham-Hodgson the Radiologist

BUCKINGHAMSHIRE

ASHLEY GREEN	*Parish Church*	Memorial to a silversmith

CORNWALL *St. Dominick Parish* Memorial 'The Rich Harvest'

ESSEX

GREAT CANFIELD	*Parish Church*	Window given by the Glaziers Company to celebrate the Mastership of Gordon Simmons Esq., 'The Six Feats of the Blessed Virgin', symbolized by seasonal flowers

HAMPSHIRE

COMPTON	*Parish Church*	'Mother and Child and Pietà'
SOUTHAMPTON	*Bitterne Park Parish Church*	Glass mosaic in Narthex, commemorating Dean Milner White

HERTFORDSHIRE

STEVENAGE	*St. George's*	East window 'The Church's Calendar'
THERFIELD	*Parish Church*	'St. Francis', memorial to a lover of birds

KENT

COBHAM	*Parish Church*	'Christ the Healer', memorial to a doctor and lover of natural history

LONDON

	St. Paul's Cathedral	Main Apse, six windows (three for *American Chapel*, three illustrating the 'I AM' texts of St. John's Gospel); *Chapel of the Order of The British Empire* (eight windows illustrating the theme 'Service', and sixteen painted glass panels incorporating portraits of the Royal Founders, Sovereigns and Grand Masters of the Order)
	Westminster Abbey	Six 'Acts of Mercy' windows in North Transept
HOLBORN	*St. Andrew's*	East window, 'The Risen and the Broken Body' Side Chapel 'Holy Ghost'
NEWGATE	*Holy Sepulchre*	Memorial windows to Dame Nellie Melba and John Ireland
REGENT'S PARK	*St. Mark's*	Memorial window to King Edward VII

LONDON (continued)

COVENT GARDEN	*St. Paul's*	Two East windows 'Titles of Christ'
FOSTER LANE	*St. Vedast's*	Three East windows 'Life of St. Vedast' to illustrate theme of 'The Civilizing Mission of the Church'
MELBURY ROAD	*Tower House*	'Zodiacal Signs' in the manner of John Burgess

MIDDLESEX

TWICKENHAM	*Parish Church*	East window 'Emblems of the Blessed Virgin'
	Fortescue House	Three East windows 'Life of St. Francis'

NORFOLK

GREAT YARMOUTH	*St. Nicholas'*	'Fishermen's window', memorial to Russell Colman Esq., Lord Lieutenant; 'Life of Christ' in East window and six other windows; 'Seven Sacraments' and 'Worthies of Yarmouth' in West windows

NORTHAMPTONSHIRE

PETERBOROUGH	*St. John's*	'Worthies of Peterborough'

SHROPSHIRE

FORD	*Parish Church*	Biographical memorial to Dr. Reginald Urwick, CC

STAFFORDSHIRE

DARLASTON	*Parish Church*	'Metaphysical Poets'
PENSNETT	*Parish Church*	'God the Maker' and 'Man the Maker', with symbols to illustrate local social, artistic and industrial activities
MEIR HEATH	*Parish Church*	Side Chapel window illustrating 'Faith responding to Grace'; West window 'The Ascension' (in progress)

SUFFOLK

CREETING	*St. Mary's Parish Church*	'The Enclosed Garden'

SCOTLAND

KIRKCUDBRIGHT

CORSOCK	*Parish Church*	'Rhododendron window', memorial to Brigadier General McEwen

ABROAD

JORDAN

JERUSALEM	*St. George's Cathedral*	'St. Mark and St. John'

NEW ZEALAND

WELLINGTON	*Cathedral*	Four War Memorial windows, six windows (in progress) illustrating the theme 'The Unknown God'

SUMNER   *Parish Church*   'Pioneers of New Zealand' given
                                                            by the New Zealand artist
                                                            Cranleigh Barton

The American Memorial Chapel, St. Paul's Cathedral, London.

Tower House, Melbury Road,
Kensington, London.

Fortescue House, Twickenham,
Middlesex.

Parish Church, Cobham, Kent.

HAMPSHIRE
SOUTHAMPTON | *Avenue Congregational Church* | 1968 | 2-light window in Chancel

YORKSHIRE
FERRYBRIDGE | *Parish Church* | 1967 | 2-light window in North Aisle

SCOTLAND

ABERDEENSHIRE
BALLATER | *St. Kentigern's Episcopal Church* | 1971 | 2-light window on North Wall (in progress)

ANGUS
DUNDEE | *St. Andrew's Parish Church* | 1967 | Single window in Gallery
| | 1971 | Two single windows in Gallery (in progress)
GLAMIS | *Parish Church* | 1969 | 2-light Nave window

AYRSHIRE
ALLOWAY | *Parish Church* | 1969 | Trefoil window in Chancel
DALMELLINGTON | *Kirk O' the Covenant* | 1971 | 2-light window in Nave (in progress)
DUNLOP | *Parish Church* | 1968 | 2-light Tower window
| | 1970 | 2-light window in Nave
SYMINGTON | *Parish Church* | 1970 | Single window in Chancel

DUNBARTONSHIRE
BEARSDEN | *South Church* | 1968 | Single window in Transept
KILLERMONT | *Parish Church* | 1966 | Two single windows in glass and concrete
| | 1969 | Two single windows in glass and concrete

EDINBURGH
| *St. Serf's Parish Church* | 1970 | Six windows in Apse
CORSTORPHINE | *Old Parish Church* | 1970 | 3-light window in Transept

GLASGOW
BELMONT | *Stevenson Memorial* | 1968 | Single Nave window
CALTON | *Parish Church* | 1970 | 3-light Chancel window
| | 1971 | Single window in Nave (in progress)
GIFFNOCK | *Orchardhill Parish Church* | 1969 | 3-light window in Transept
| *South Parish Church* | 1971 | 2-light window in Transept (in progress)
| | 1971 | 3-light window in Nave (in progress)
KELVINSIDE | *Lansdowne Parish Church* | 1966 | Single window in North Gallery
| *St. John's Renfield* | 1967 | Single window in Nave
| | 1970 | Single window in Nave
SHETTLESTON | *Old Parish Church* | 1967 | Single window in North Aisle
| | 1971 | Single window in progress

Opposite
Old Parish Church, Corstorphine, Edinburgh. 'The Dual Baptism — by water and by the Holy Spirit'.

GLASGOW (continued)

UNIVERSITY	*Bute Hall*	1970	5-light armorial window
WHITEINCH	*Victoria Park Church*	1970	Two single glass in concrete windows on West Wall
NEWLANDS	*St. Margaret's Episcopal*	1971	Single window in progress

INVERNESS-SHIRE

INVERNESS	*Ness Bank Church*	1967	2-light window in Nave
SPEAN BRIDGE	*Kilmonivaig Parish Church*	1967	Two single windows in Chancel

LANARKSHIRE

MOTHERWELL	*South Dalziel Church*	1968	2-light window in Nave
	St. Mary's Parish Church	1968	Three single windows in vestibule
NEW MONKLAND	*Old Parish Church*	1969	Single window in Nave
HAMILTON	*St. Andrew's Church*	1971	2-light window in Nave (in progress)

PERTHSHIRE

DUNBLANE	*Cathedral*	1968	4-light window in Nave
CRIEFF	*St. Andrew's Church*	1969	Two single windows in vestibule
		1971	Three single windows in Nave (in progress)
PERTH	*St. John's Episcopal Church*	1970	Single window in Transept

RENFREWSHIRE

BARRHEAD	*Arthurlie Church*	1967	West window. Heavy glass in epoxy resin

STIRLINGSHIRE

GRANGEMOUTH	*Old Parish Church*	1966	3-light window in Nave
KIPPEN	*Parish Church*	1971	2-light window in Nave (in progress)

EIRE

CO. CORK

KINSALE	*St. Multose Church*	1969	2-light window in Transept

ABROAD

BERMUDA

HAMILTON	*Christ Church*	1967	Single window in West Wall
		1971	Single window in Nave (in progress

Opposite

Bute Hall, Glasgow University. Subject — Arms of former Rectors of the University.

A CARRICK WHALEN, FMGP
Studio House, 60a Dean Path, Edinburgh

SCOTLAND

DUNBARTONSHIRE
CLYDEBANK *Clydebank Crematorium* 1966 Single-light window, artificially lit 'Figure of the Resurrection'

INVERNESS-SHIRE
FORT WILLIAM *Duncansburgh Parish Church* 1969 Rose window 'Last Supper'

MIDLOTHIAN
ROSLIN *Roslin Chapel* 1970 Single-light window 'St. Francis'

STIRLINGSHIRE
RAPLOCH *St. Mark's Church* 1960–61 Two single-light windows for Guides and Brownies Jubilee year

1966 Panel 'The Lion of St. Mark'

STIRLING *St. Mark's Church* 1969 Single-light window artificially lit 'St. Martha'

Roslin Chapel, Roslin, Midlothian, Scotland.

WHITEFRIARS STAINED GLASS STUDIOS
Alfred R. Fisher, FMGP
Tudor Road, Wealdstone, Middlesex

BEDFORDSHIRE

BIDDENHAM	*Parish Church*	1969	2-light Chancel window
BEDFORD	*Harpur Trust Almshouses*	1970	Rearrangement of old glass

BUCKINGHAMSHIRE

LITTLE HORWOOD	*Horwood House*	1970	Reglazing

CHESHIRE

GREAT BUDWORTH	*Parish Church*	1965	Several windows
CHEADLE	*Christ Church, Heald Green*	1971	Font in fused and cast glass

CORNWALL

*TINTAGEL	*Parish Church*	1968	3-light Heraldic window

DEVONSHIRE

PLYMOUTH	*St. Alban's Garrison Church*	1966–69	Three single-light windows

ESSEX

*BIRDBROOK	*Parish Church*	1966–70	Several windows
*KIRBY-LE-SOKEN	*St. Michael's Church*	1969–70	Two 3-light windows
STAMBRIDGE	*Parish Church*	1971	2-light window

GLOUCESTERSHIRE

BADMINTON	*Petty France Hotel*	1970	Architectural Glass Screen
CINDERFORD	*Wesleyan Church*	1969	2-light window

HERTFORDSHIRE

CUFFLEY	*St. Andrew's Church*	1965–66	Thirteen fused glass windows

KENT

PETTS WOOD	*Lutheran Church*	1968	Single-light window

LANCASHIRE

LIVERPOOL	*Childwall Parish Church*	1968	2-light window
BOOTLE	*Trustee Savings Bank*	1969	Fused glass feature

LINCOLNSHIRE

NETTLEHAM	*Parish Church*	1970	Restoration work

LONDON

OAKWOOD	*St. Thomas' Church*	1965	5-light Lady Chapel window
STAINES	*United Glass Limited*	1965	Fused glass Screen in Showrooms
EARLS COURT	*St. Philip's Church*	1966	East window
STRAND, WC	*Royal Courts of Justice*	1967	5-light Heraldic window
KENSINGTON	*St. Mary Abbot's Church*	1967	2-light window
EALING	*St. David's Home*	1967	Circular window
SOMERSTOWN	*St. Aloysius' Church*	1967	Clerestory and Baptistery windows
LONDON, EC	*Stationers' Hall*	1967	Releading and repairs
*EUSTON ROAD	*Elizabeth Garratt-Anderson Hospital*	1968	Single-light window
SWISS COTTAGE	*St. Thomas More Church*	1968	Large Sanctuary window
ST. JAMES' PALACE	*Queen's Chapel*	1968	East window
*EASTCOTE	*St. Lawrence Church*	1968	East window
HARROW	*St. John's Church, Greenhill*	1968	2-light window

LONDON (continued)

GREENFORD — *Rockware Glass Limited* — 1970 — Fused glass mural in Research Centre

NOTTINGHAMSHIRE

WEST BRIDGFORD — *St. Giles' Church* — 1971 — 4-light window

SOMERSET

BATHFORD — *St. Swithun's Church* — 1970 — Restoration of fire damage

STAFFORDSHIRE

WALL HEATH — *Church of the Ascension* — 1969 — 4-light window
★KNYPERSLEY — *Parish Church* — 1970 — Single-light window

SUFFOLK

LITTLE GLEMHAM — *Parish Church* — 1970 — Single-light window
★BURY ST. EDMUNDS — *St. Mary's Church* — 1970 — Single-light window

WARWICKSHIRE

★BIRMINGHAM — *Quinton Parish Church* — 1966 — Single-light window

YORKSHIRE

★LEEDS — *St. Edmund's Church, Roundhay* — 1969 — Two 2-light windows
LOW BENTHAM — *Parish Church* — 1970 — 2-light window

SCOTLAND

LOCHSIDE — *St. Ninian's Church* — 1966 — Five appliqué windows

CHANNEL ISLANDS

JERSEY

ST. HELIER — *St. James' Church* — 1970 — Several windows

ABROAD

CANADA

DORVAL — *United Church* — 1966 — Several windows
MONTREAL — *Ceylon Pavilion Expo '67* — 1966 — Mural

ICELAND

REYKJAVIK — *'Rima' Shop* — 1966 — Fused Panel
KEFLAVIK — *Church* — 1969 — Circular window

NEPAL

KATMANDU — *Royal Palace* — 1968 — Three windows

NEW ZEALAND

★REMUERA — *St. Mark's Church* — 1967 — Several windows
AUCKLAND — ★*St. Matthew's Church* — 1967 — Two 2-light windows
Methodist Central Mission — 1968 — West Front window
★HASTINGS — *St. Matthew's Church* — 1970 — West window

SOUTH AFRICA

★DURBAN — *Holy Trinity Church* — 1967 — 3-light window
★STELLENBOSCH — *St. Mary's Church* — 1967 — Single-light window
MEERHOF — *Children's Hospital Chapel* — 1968 — Two single-light windows
★JOHANNESBURG — *St. Francis' Church* — 1968–70 — Several windows

U.S.A.

PITTSBURGH	*St. Bernard Church, Mt. Lebanon*	1965–68	All windows
PALISADES PARK	*Zion Lutheran Church*	1967	West window
*SHORT HILLS	*Christ Church*	1967	Several windows
NEW YORK	*St. Thomas's Church, Fifth Avenue*	1970	5-light window
*SUMMIT, N.J.	*Calvary Episcopal Church*	1966–71	Several windows
*EVANSTON, ILL.	*St. Luke's Church*	1969	2-light window in Lady Chapel

*Designed by Rupert Moore, ARCA, FMGP.

SLAB GLASS IN EPOXY RESIN OR CONCRETE
Alfred Fisher, FMGP

DURHAM CO.

CROFT	*St. Cuthbert's Hospital Chapel*	1971	Glazing of whole Chapel

LONDON

EASTCHEAP	*Millocrat House*	1969	Epoxy resin mural in reception area

Pierre Fourmaintraux, FMGP

BUCKINGHAMSHIRE

SLOUGH	*Methodist Church*	1965	Three large windows

CHESHIRE

LEASOWE	*St. Chad's Church*	1965	Four windows

DEVONSHIRE

PLYMOUTH	*Weston Mill Crematorium*	1966	Three windows

DORSET

BULFORD CAMP	*R.C. Chapel*	1968	West window

HERTFORDSHIRE

CHESHUNT	*Western Synagogue Cemetery*	1967	All windows

LANCASHIRE

MANCHESTER	*St. Augustine's Church*	1966	Lancet windows
LIVERPOOL	*Childwall Methodist Church*	1968	Four windows
FAZAKERLEY	*Hospital Chapel*	1971	Two windows

LINCOLNSHIRE

LINCOLN	*Crematorium*	1968	Eight windows

LONDON

HESTON	*Church of Our Lady, Queen of Apostles*	1966	Windows in Baptistery
NORTHOLT	*St. Hugh's Church*	1970	Altar window

NOTTINGHAMSHIRE

KEYWORTH	*Mary Ward College*	1967	Large Chapel windows

SURREY

GUILDFORD	*Crematorium*	1966	Chapel windows
EWELL	*Chapel of Rest*	1969	Single window

SUSSEX

EASTBOURNE	*Church of Our Lady of Ransom*	1967	2-light window
CRAWLEY	*St. Peter's Church, West Green*	1969	3-light West window

YORKSHIRE

SHEFFIELD	*St. Luke's Church, Lodgemoor*	1966	Three windows
BRACEWELL	*Parish Church*	1967	Small window

SCOTLAND

GLASGOW	*'Lunar 7'*	1967	Concrete Façade
AYR	*Masonhill Crematorium*	1965	Two windows
LINWOOD	*High School*	1965	One window

WALES

GLAMORGANSHIRE

CARDIFF	*University Chapel*	1968	Windows in Lecture Hall
MARGAM	*Crematorium*	1968	Ten windows

PEMBROKESHIRE

NARBERTH	*Crematorium*	1967	Frame and window units

NORTHERN IRELAND

BELFAST	*Methodist College Chapel*	1968	Four large windows

NEW ZEALAND

SYDENHAM-BECKENHAM CHRISTCHURCH	*St. Saviour's Church*	1966	Three windows

Church of the Ascension, Wall Heath, Staffordshire. Design by Alfred Fisher.

Right
St. Aloysius' Church, Somerstown, London.
Design by Paul Jeffries.

Left
Winthrop Memorial Window,
Stambridge Church, Essex.
Design by Alfred Fisher.

St. Thomas' Church, Oakwood, London. Design by Alfred Fisher.

Left
'Rosary Window' —
St. John's and St. Patrick's
Cathedral, Newfoundland,
Canada.
Design by Rupert Moore.

Below
St. Alban's Garrison Church,
Plymouth, Devonshire.
Design by Alfred Fisher.

ROY E. YOUNGS, MGP
28 White Horse Drive, Epsom, Surrey

ESSEX

SOUTH WOODFORD	*United Free Church*	1963	Resin and glass mural with Lawrence Lee
HARLOW	*St. John's School House*	1970	Heraldic window

LANCASHIRE

MANCHESTER	*Whitefield Synagogue*	1969–70	Twelve windows of twelve Tribes of Israel. With Modern Art Glass Co.

LONDON

MAYFAIR	*Office of C.P.V.*	1970	Sand blasted/etched heraldic panel
GREAT ORMOND STREET	*Hospital Chapel*	1967	Heraldic panel. With John Stevens
KENNINGTON	*Private House*	1968	Restoration of two William Morris windows
	Private House	1965	Single-light Madonna window
KENSINGTON	*St. Stephen's*	1964	Restoration pieces of twenty windows
KING'S CROSS	*Station Bar*	1964	Mosaic
NORWOOD	*Crematorium, Private Chapels*	1967	Restoration of two windows

YORKSHIRE

HALIFAX	*Grammar School*	1966	Two Heraldic windows, with Modern Art Glass Co.
LEEDS	*Church of the Sacred Heart*	1965	Glass and resin mural, with Lawrence Lee
RIPLEY	*Castle*	1967–70	Heraldic windows restoration with Modern Art Glass Co.
SHEFFIELD	*Cathedral, Chapel*	1970	Heraldic window, with Keith New

ABROAD

U.S.A.

SYRACUSE, N.Y.	*Private House*	1967	Two panels, with Richard Woolf

INDEX OF BRITISH COUNTIES, MAJOR CITIES AND COUNTRIES ABROAD
For example – for Alberta, Ontario, see under Canada
For Madingley see Cambridgeshire
Page Numbers in **bold** represent illustration pages

119

Nepal	P112	Warwickshire	P6, 11, **12**, 35, 38, **38**, 41,
New Zealand	P11, **11**, 20, 37, 48, 64, **64**,		47, 56, 57, **59**, 60, 64, 70,
	72, 87, 89, 102, 103, 112,		72, 86, 89, 95, 112
	114	West Indies	P17, 48
Nigeria	P37	Westmorland	P47, 90
Norfolk	P19, **30**, 35, 40, **42**, 63,	Wiltshire	P6, 47, 57, 80
	85, 88, **89**, 102	Worcestershire	P6, 47, 49, 57, 89, 92
North Africa	P20		
Northamptonshire	P5, 6, **7**, 19, 35, 38, 55,	Yorkshire	P11, **12**, 19, **23**, 30, 37, 41,
	60, 63, 70, 85, 86, 102		47, 52, 57, 60, 61, 70, **71**,
Northern Ireland	P19, 31, 37, 64, 90, 114		72, 80, **81**, 82, 86, 89, **91**,
Northumberland	P55, 70		92, 95, 96, **97**, 106, 112,
Nottinghamshire	P35, 44, **44**, 47, 55, 86,		114, 118
	92, 95, 112, 113		

Oxfordshire   P35, 63, 70, 80, 86, 88

Pembrokeshire   P15, 114
Perthshire   P108

Radnorshire   P15, 61
Renfrewshire   P57, 96, 108
Rhodesia   P20
Rutland   P88

St. Helena   See 'South Atlantic'
Scilly Isles   P41
Scotland   P39, 57, 58, **59**, 96, 102,
106, **107**, 108, **109**, 110,
114
Shropshire   P24, 55, 95, 102
Somerset   P5, 13, 35, 38, 52, **53**, 56,
112
South Africa   P11, 17, 20, 48, 52, 64,
72, 82, 87, 96, 112
South Atlantic   P20
Staffordshire   P13, 19, 30, 47, 56, **58**,
60, 78, 82, 86, 90, 92,
102, 112, **114**
Stirlingshire   P108, 110
Suffolk   P30, 35, 47, 56, 60, 95,
102, 112
Surrey   P6, 19, **23**, 35, 40, 41, 47,
56, 64, 70, **71**, 73, 80, 82,
88, 95, 114
Sussex   P6, 8, 19, 35, 41, 47, 49,
51, 70, 78, 80, 82, 86, 88,
92, 95, 114
Switzerland   P6

Tanzania   P37, 64
Trinidad   P72
Tunisia   P48

Uganda   P20
U.S.A. (America)   P1, **1**, 17, 21, 22, **22**, 25,
26, **27**, **28**, 29, 43, **43**, 48,
78, **79**, 87, 98, **98**, **99**,
100, 113, 118

Wales   P20, 24, 31, 48, 57, 61,
72, 78, 80, 87, 90, 96, 114